T.
Post

BOLTON
WANDERERS

IVAN PONTING
BARRY HUGMAN

Copyright: Repvern Publishing

Published in Great Britain by Repvern Publishing, Millway House, Knole,
Long Sutton, Langport, Somerset TA10 9HY

Designed and typeset by Bob Bickerton

Additional typesetting by Jean Baston

Printed and bound in Great Britain by Hillman Printers (Frome) Ltd, Frome, Somerset.

Trade Sales and distribution: Little Red Witch Books 0823 490080

ISBN 1-869833-27-9

Probably Bolton's finest hour in the post-war era. Nat Lofthouse shows the FA Cup to the delighted Trotter fans.

The FA Cup holders pictured early in 1958-59 : Back row, left to right: Bill Ridding, (manager), Roy Hartle, Derek Hennin, Eddie Hopkinson, Gordon Edwards, John Higgins, Brian Edwards, Bert Sproston, (trainer).
Front row, left to right: Bryan Birch, Dennis Stevens, Nat Lofthouse, Mr W H Warburton, (chairman), Ray Parry, Doug Holden and Tommy Banks.

CONTENTS

Throughout the book there are statistical records of all Bolton players who have played in the Football League since 1946-47. See key below.

Name ———————— **BIRCH, Brian** ———————— Signing -on date
Date and place of birth ——— *Southport, 9 April, 1938* ——— League appearances
 ┌— Bolton W   4.55 165   0 23 └— Substitute appearances
Clubs played for ——— └— Rochdale   7.64   60   1   6 ┐— League goals

Nat Lofthouse, hero for the publisher and thousands of other boys in the 1950s.

INTRODUCTION

'I hope you realise that constantly thumping your head like that can damage your brain!'

That was the warning a worried schoolmaster gave me after watching in horror as I dived recklessly around the penalty area, choosing to head the ball at every opportunity rather than use my feet.

Of course, he meant well; but he didn't realise I was Nat Lofthouse!

To me, as to thousands of other football-mad youngsters in the early 1950s, 'The Lion of Vienna' was the ultimate role model. The thrilling way he led the forward lines of both Bolton Wanderers and England was nothing short of an inspiration to all of us.

Nat is still an important personality at Burnden Park, and he was obviously intensely proud in the spring of 1994 as the Trotters enjoyed their second consecutive giant-killing run in the FA Cup.

In the past Bolton have enjoyed their glamour days at Wembley and their mammoth attendances in the old First Division. As a result they are blessed with avid supporters all over the world, loyal supporters who are watching and waiting to see them return at the top.

I believe this book, which features all the best-known Trotters since the war, will bring hours of enjoyment to all who cherish the Burnden cause.

As its publisher, whose love of football was confirmed so memorably and irrevocably by Nat Lofthouse's six goals (including four headers!) for the Football League at Molineux in 1952, I hope, in particular, that it will be relished by the club president.

Tony Williams
Publisher

Bolton Wanderers
. . . the very
name
resounds with the
proudest traditions and
headiest romance of
English football,
courtesy of an eventful
history dating back to
1877. Founder members
of the Football League
11 years later, the
Trotters have never
lifted that coveted
trophy but, come the
watershed of the Second
World War, they could
point to three FA Cup
triumphs - all in the
1920s - and had built up
a large and devoted local
following.

As the clouds of
conflict rolled away,
football was to play a
hugely significant social
role. Though it was a
time of national
austerity, people were
out to enjoy themselves
after six years of horror
and deprivation, and the
game offered a dramatic,
accessible and generally
affordable diversion.

Bolton were well placed
to play their part. In
1945 they beat Chelsea
to win the Wartime Cup,
finished a creditable

*The sight that stunned the whole of Bolton and the rest
of the footballing world; shocked faces in the Burnden
Park crowd look on as the bodies of the injured and
dying are assembled on the pitch.*

ninth in the northern
section of the Wartime
League and in
rumbustious young
centre-forward Nat
Lofthouse they
possessed one of the
most exciting prospects
in the land.

Yet barely had peace
broken out when the

country was rocked by
the worst tragedy in
British sporting history
to date, and it was born
out of the prevailing
hunger for high-quality
entertainment.

In the absence of a
fully-fledged League
competition in 1945/46
the Football Association

BATTLES

decreed that Cup ties up to and including the quarter-finals should be played on a two-leg basis. Bolton progressed impressively to the last eight, where they beat Stoke City 2-0 at the Victoria Ground in the first leg.

With Stanley Matthews, then acknowledged as the world's greatest footballer, in the Stoke line-up and with the Trotters hot favourites to reach the semi-finals, it seemed that the whole of Bolton was intent on turning up at Burnden Park for the return encounter on March 9. In the event, the official attendance figure stood at 65,419, but an estimated 85,000 attempted to gain admittance on what was to prove one of the blackest days the cotton town had ever known.

Twenty-five minutes before kick-off, the terraces were packed by a heaving mass of fans, many unable to move of their own volition but frequently being swept along helplessly by the frightening crush. Quite simply, the ground was full but still people poured in, some of them climbing over belatedly closed turnstiles.

One small boy in the embankment enclosure became distressed and his father, desperate for escape, picked the padlock of an exit gate and the pair squeezed to safety. Disastrously, many more charged through the gateway and pushed forward against those already inside. As the teams ran out, two barriers collapsed and supporters trapped near the front were hurled to the ground by the sudden resultant surge from behind.

Though hundreds were trampled, the scale of the accident was not immediately apparent and the match started on time. Players saw bodies

stretched out on the running track but assumed that people had merely fainted. Soon, though, it became clear that lives had been lost and the game was stopped.

Even then, with efficient communication impossible in an atmosphere of bedlam, the majority of supporters were unaware of the calamity and the police, fearing even greater carnage, asked the referee to resume the match, which he did after a 15-minute break.

The final toll was 33 dead and around 500 injured. The town - indeed, the nation - was stunned and a relief fund quickly raised nearly £40,000, a huge sum in those days. The Home Office immediately set up an inquiry, which criticised some aspects of spectator control and communication, but concluded that, in effect, the crowd had inflicted the disaster on itself. As a result, £5,500 worth of improvements were made to the embankment and a few new safety regulations were introduced for all grounds, but the potential for further, even larger-scale tragedies was not remotely appreciated. This is astonishing, and not only in the light of subsequent happenings at Ibrox and Hillsborough. As far back as 1923 there had been a graphic warning at the famous 'White Horse' FA Cup Final, the first at Wembley, in which Bolton beat West

STAN HANSON
1936/37 - 1955/56

Poor Stan Hanson. To so many people, his name conjures up visions of one shaky performance, for Bolton against Blackpool in the 1953 FA Cup Final. Unfortunately for the long-serving goalkeeper, that game - known universally as 'The Matthews Final' - remains one of the most famous and pored-over sporting contests of the century and his mistakes have been highlighted on film again and again all over the world. In fact, that is grossly unfair to a well-respected custodian whose top-flight career with the Trotters spanned 20 years and to whom he gave splendid service either side of the war. Bootle-born Stan, who became famed for his long-distance kicking, had amateur experience with both Liverpool and Southport before spurning overtures from Aston Villa to turn professional with the Wanderers in October 1935. It was not until 1938/39 that he won a regular first-team place, and then his progress was interrupted by the hostilities, during which he served side by side with a dozen of his Bolton team-mates in the Royal Artillery. He played plenty of high-grade wartime football before resuming his career in 1945, his consistent form over five seasons being recognised by selection for an FA tour of Canada in 1950. Perhaps Stan remained the Trotters' first choice a little too long - until 1955, his 40th year - and towards the end of his reign he tended to be vulnerable on crosses. On retirement, he maintained his association with the club by coaching the 'B' team, and also ran the post office near the ground until he retired in 1986. Stan, whose brother Alf played for Liverpool and Chelsea, died the following year.

WILLIE MOIR
1945/46 - 1955/56

The name of Willie Moir looms large in the post-war history of Bolton Wanderers. The strong, skilful Scot joined the Trotters in 1943 and over the next dozen years turned out in every forward position. Though right-footed, he was an effective left-winger, but he was most acomplished as a goal-scoring inside-right, a berth in which he was an ideal partner of Nat Lofthouse. Willie was at his most rampant in 1948/49 when, entrusted with the number-eight shirt in the season's fourth game at Villa Park, he responded by netting four times, including a penalty. He retained the position for the rest of the season, which he finished as the First Division's leading scorer with 25 goals. Thereafter he was never quite so prolific again, though consecutive senior tallies of 16, 22 and 23 from 1951/52 to 1953/54 bore testimony to his value as secondary marksman to Nat. Though not the swiftest of movers, Willie was splendid in the air for a fairly small man and was well endowed with ball skills, a combination which endeared him enormously to the Burnden crowd. He was a natural leader, too, a well-respected captain who led the side into the 1953 FA Cup Final against Blackpool. That day he battled enterprisingly and when Bolton led 3-1 it seemed, wrongly, that Willie's would be the hands to lift the trophy. He found himself on the scoresheet, too, though film of the match suggests that he never got his head to Bobby Langton's cross and that the goal should have been credited to the winger. In 1955 Willie, the last Trotter to win a Scottish cap before John McGinlay, moved to Stockport, whom he served as player-boss. Later he worked as a salesman, but never severed his connection with Burnden, where he remained a familiar face until shortly before he died in 1988.

ALLARDYCE, Samuel (Sam)
Dudley, 19 October, 1954

Bolton W.	11.71	180	4	21
Sunderland	07.80	24	1	2
Millwall	09.81	63	0	2
Coventry C.	09.83	28	0	1
Huddersfield T.	07.84	37	0	0
Bolton W.	07.85	14	0	0
Preston N.E.	08.86	88	2	2
West Bromwich A.	06.89	0	1	0
Preston N.E. (N/C)	08.92	1	2	0

ALLCOCK, Terence
Leeds, 10 December, 1935

Bolton W.	12.52	31	0	9
Norwich C.	03.58	334	5	106

ALLEN, Paul R.
Bury, 13 March, 1968

Bolton W.	07.86	0	1	0

ASPINALL, John
Aston-under-Lyne, 27 April, 1916

Oldham Ath.	05.36	11	0	0
Bolton W.	09.45	14	0	0

ATKINSON, John Edward
Washington, 20 December, 1913

Bolton W.	09.31	240	0	4
New Brighton	05.48	52	0	0

ATKINSON, Paul Graham
Pudsey, 14 August, 1961

Oldham Ath.	08.79	139	4	11
Watford	07.83	8	3	0
Oldham Ath.	08.85	29	4	1
Swansea C.	12.86	6	0	1
Bolton W.	02.87	2	1	0
Swansea C.	03.87	12	0	2
Burnley	07.88	18	4	1

BAILEY, Dennis
Biddulph, 24 September, 1935

Bolton W.	09.53	1	0	0
Port Vale	08.58	1	0	0

BAILEY, Ian Craig
Middlesbrough, 20 October, 1956

Middlesbrough	10.74	140	4	1
Doncaster Rov.	11.76	9	0	0
Carlisle U.	02.77	7	0	1
Bolton W.	11.81	5	0	0
Sheffield Wed.	08.82	35	0	0
Blackpool	10.8	3	0	0
Bolton W.	03.8	10	0	0

BALL, John
Wigan, 13 March, 1925

Manchester U.	03.48	22	0	0
Bolton W.	09.50	200	0	2

BANKS, Ralph
Farnworth, 28 June, 1920   Died 1993

Bolton W.	12.40	104	0	0
Aldershot	01.54	43	0	1

BANKS, Thomas
Farnworth, 10 November, 1929

Bolton W.	10.47	233	0	2

Ham United. That game attracted a gate of more than 126,000, plus some 70,000 more who invaded the stadium without paying; that there were no fatalities as mayhem reigned was little short of miraculous.

To return to the Burnden Park incident, the outcome of the tie could hardly matter in such heart-rending circumstances but, for the record, the second leg ended scoreless and Bolton reached the last four, only to lose 2-0 to Charlton Athletic at Villa Park.

Of course, though such trauma left inevitable scars, life went on for the Trotters. The Football League restarted on August 31 1946 and Bolton kicked off, thrillingly if unsuccessfully, by losing to Chelsea at Stamford Bridge by the odd goal in seven. Two of the Lancastrians' three were netted by Lofthouse, a telling pointer to the years ahead.

Managed diligently by their former player and coach Walter Rowley, Bolton won four of their next five games to fuel hopes that they could become one of the first post-war footballing powers. Sadly their performances slumped and they slid alarmingly down the table, eventually finishing 18th, though relegation was avoided by nine points.

With their title hopes dead by Christmas, the focus turned to the FA Cup, in which the club had a commendable

MALCOLM BARRASS 1946/47 - 1956/57

Malcolm Barrass was a thoroughbred footballer. The son of a former pro - his father, Matt, played for Blackpool, Sheffield Wednesday and Manchester City between the wars - he lived for the game from an early age, and it showed. Having spurned the advances of Wolves to sign for Bolton, he impressed as a free-scoring inside-forward during wartime competition and was rewarded by selection for an England Victory international in 1945. Sometimes he wore the number-nine shirt, and when he netted four in that role at home to Manchester City in November 1948, it seemed reasonable to think that his future would be as a spearhead. But the Trotters boasted a certain young man called Lofthouse, and such was Malcolm's versatility that he was capable of doing well in almost any position. Eventually he gravitated to the half-back line, his cool, cultured approach meshing ideally with the more vigorous methods of his defensive colleagues. At first the tall left-footer was deployed at wing-half, where his passing skills and reading of the game were at a premium, but later he took on the central role which he occupied in the 1953 FA Cup Final against Blackpool. That day he was handed the unenviable task of subduing the effervescent Stanley Mortensen and, despite Stan's hat-trick, Malcolm did not give a bad performance. At the time he was the current England centre-half (he won three full caps), a tribute to his consistent form in what was probably his finest season. Malcolm left Burnden for Sheffield United in 1956, later entering the non-League ranks. Always he remained a student of the game, the sort who would kick every ball over again as he reviewed his contribution after the match. Over the years, that dedication had paid rich dividends.

NAT LOFTHOUSE
1945/46 - 1960/61

If visitors from another planet, intrigued by the devotion of earthlings to their curious game of soccer, should hear the phrase 'traditional, old-fashioned English centre-forward' and want to know more, they would be well advised to study film of Nat Lofthouse in action. Better still, should these aliens have the facility of time travel and be able to return to the 1950s when the 'Lion of Vienna' was in his roaring prime, they could experience the real thing, a true working-class hero in all his vigorous glory.

As talismanic and constant a figure to his beloved Bolton as is his friend and England colleague Tom Finney to fellow Lancastrians Preston North End, Lofthouse embodied football's most simple virtues. Whether wearing the white shirt of club or country, he toiled mightily, the archetypal human battering ram who plundered his goals - hundreds of them down the years - through prodigious strength, aggression and courage, his dynamic aerial power backed up by a savage shot in either foot.

Of course, though Nat himself is too modest to admit it, there was more to it than that. What marked him out from the typical hard-running English workhorse was an instinct for making the absolute most of his yeoman qualities. Muscle and sweat might have taken Nat Lofthouse a long way in his chosen profession, but not to the heady peaks he ascended, including a record-equalling 30 goals in 33 international appearances.

Significant, too, in the creation of a widely revered persona, was (and is) his down-to-earth attitude. Essentially a humble man who felt privileged to be paid for pleasure - his own view of his working contract - he was born in Bolton and has lived his whole life there. Lofthouse loves the local community; indeed, he has taken such an active part in it while performing his various roles with Wanderers - first player, then trainer, coach, manager, scout, fund-raiser and president - that he has come to epitomise it.

Though the town was famous for wool and cotton, it was coal that loomed largest in the Lofthouse household in the 1920s. Nat's father delivered the stuff with a horse and cart, and when the youngest of four boys was old enough to earn a living, he did so pushing tubs in the local pit.

But football had always been his passion, from the days when he had played truant from school to shin up a drainpipe at Burnden Park to snatch a free view of his heroes in action. Ironically his first organised game was as a goalkeeper - the very breed of which he would one day become a scourge - and he conceded seven goals, injury being added to insult as he received a hiding from his mother for scuffing his new shoes in the process. Soon, though, he found his spiritual home at centre-forward, later observing cheerfully that he didn't have the brains to be anything else, and scored seven times on his debut for Bolton Schools.

In 1939 his prowess was recognised

when he joined Wanderers as an amateur and, with so many footballers away at war, he played his first senior match a year later at the tender age of 15. However, as he grew towards maturity there was very little tender about the Lofthouse physique. Though he stood only a shade over 5ft 9in, he was blessed with a burly, four-square frame hardened by labour below ground, and before he turned professional in 1942 - on wages of £1.10s (£1.50p) per week - he needed ever ounce of stamina. A typical match-day schedule for the Bolton 'Bevin boy' was to rise at 3.30am, take the 4.30 tram to work, spend eight hours down the pit, then turn out for the Trotters in the afternoon.

Yet at first, despite earning respect as

a trier and contributing a creditable goal tally, Lofthouse suffered terrace criticism for lack of technique. Though admitting disarmingly to natural clumsiness, he persevered and as soccer resumed normality after the conflict he matured gradually into one of the country's top spearheads.

Reward came in November 1950 with his first England cap, and he responded with two goals in a 2-2 draw with Yugoslavia at Highbury. That was but a foretaste of international success to come, none more lauded than the 1952 performance that earned him the 'Lion of Vienna' tag. Austria had a wonderful side at the time and expected to beat England soundly, but late in the second half of a tempestuous encounter the score was 2-2, Lofthouse having netted once. Then, with the home side pressing for a winner, Tom Finney put Nat through on goal; with a pack of defenders on his heels and the crowd baying wildly, he kept his head to clip the ball into the net even as he was clattered by the charging goalkeeper. Such was the impact of the collision that he was stretchered off, returning later to share in the final moments of a 3-2 triumph before being chaired around

the ground by an ecstatic contingent of British troops, then stationed nearby.

That year Bolton turned down an approach for his services from the Italian club, Fiorentina, who offered a deal that would have made Lofthouse rich beyond his dreams. Such was the one-sided nature of club-player relationships in

that era that he was never offered the chance to decide for himself, though he maintained that the iniquitous situation never bothered him - it was just a fact of life and, as he felt himself to be immeasurably better off than the average working man, he was not going to make waves.

So Lofthouse continued to serve the Burnden Park

cause nobly, and was their most eye-catching performer in two memorable FA Cup Finals. First in 1953, as the reigning Footballer of the Year (right), he gave Wanderers a two-minute lead over Blackpool, then saw his side draw 3-1 ahead, only for the great Stanley Matthews to turn the contest on its head and inspire a late victory for the Seasiders.

But in 1958 Nat, by then the captain, was not to be denied. Refusing to be affected by the understandable sentimentality surrounding their opponents - a Manchester United side ravaged so cruelly by the Munich air crash only three months earlier - he scored both goals in a 2-0 victory, including the controversial second, described in detail elsewhere in this book.

Having played in the 1954 World Cup Finals, Lofthouse was overlooked for the 1958 tournament, though he was recalled later that year and equalled Finney's England scoring record, since passed by Bobby Charlton. In addition, he once netted six times for the Football League against the League of Ireland, realising the classic boyhood fantasy of a hat-trick in each half.

Come 1960, aged 35 and bothered by niggling knee and ankle injuries, he retired to become Wanderers' reserve team trainer. Having been very much the main attraction, with 285 goals in 503 club outings, he did not relish the prospect of sweeping floors and cleaning boots, which the job entailed, but so loth was he to leave Burnden that he accepted it.

In 1968, with Bolton short of money and having slipped out of the First Division, Lofthouse took over as manager. It was a move he was to regret, later declaring: 'I was the worst manager in the world.' Though he got on well with his players, he was a natural worrier and was not good at taking the tougher decisions, and in November 1970 he stepped aside to take a purely administrative role. Amazingly, before the

season's end he had served two more stints as caretaker boss, first Jimmy McIlroy and then Jimmy Meadows shifting quickly from the hot seat.

As loyal as ever, Lofthouse became Bolton's chief scout in May 1971, glad to be shot of the cares of top office and happy to retain an important job. However, he was not judged successful in the post and a year later came the rudest shock of his life to date - he was sacked.

Then, for six years, his only connection with the club he symbolised was as a supporter, before he returned to take on the task of fund-raising figurehead, running the Burnden Executive Club. Surprisingly, December 1985 brought another spell as caretaker boss - albeit for only one match - and in 1986 he was elevated to the status of club president. Distraught at the death of his wife Alma in 1985, Lofthouse needed to keep himself busy, and did so in his new position, forever willing and able to promote the clubs's good name. How appropriate that appointment was; after all, to countless fans all over the world, Nat Lofthouse *is* Bolton Wanderers.

pedigree, but there was to be little joy on the knockout front, either. After comfortably disposing of humble Stockport County, the Trotters managed only a draw at home to Manchester City, before bowing out by the only goal at Maine Road.

That season set a dismal precedent for the immediate future. In each of the next three campaigns, demotion was an ever-present spectre, banished only in late spring. In the FA Cup Bolton fared no better, failing to

BOBBY LANGTON 1949/50 - 1952/53

When Bolton paid Preston a club-record £20,000 for Bobby Langton in November 1949, the England international left-winger was marginally past his prime yet still a fine player. Though a measure of his former pace had gone, he made up for it with wily tactical acumen that created space for himself and his left-flank team-mates. Bobby was the ball's master. He could use it with delicate finesse to open a defence with a single pinpoint pass, or dispatch it with thunderous power if a shot was on. He was ever aware of the changing options in a game and had a knack of selecting the right one. A speciality was the driven head-high cross, a chaos-inducing weapon which created numerous goals for Nat Lofthouse and Willie Moir. A forthright character, Bobby was a confirmed talker on the field and always stood up for players' rights off it in an era when so many footballers tended to be seen and not heard. Indeed, he was in dispute with the club during the run-up to the 1953 FA Cup Final, in which he made a goal for Moir with a teasing chip. The following September, by then 35, Bobby rejoined his first club, Blackburn Rovers, whom he served for three further seasons before joining Ards in Northern Ireland, where he had played for Glentoran in 1945. Later he played for and coached a succession of non-League clubs back in England, taking over as manager of his hometown team, Burscough Rangers, in 1968. With his talent, his nous and his strong personality, Bobby Langton epitomised much that was best about Lancashire football.

progress beyond the fourth round each time, though there was the minor consolation of winning the fiercely contested Lancashire Cup in 1948, a feat they have yet to repeat.

But if the side was struggling, there was at least some individual success to cause rejoicing among Burnden Park regulars. Despite a few stutters in form, Lofthouse, soon to star for England, continued to build a formidable reputation as a marksman, while his

JOHNNY WHEELER 1950/51 - 1955/56

Johnny Wheeler was the quiet man of Burnden Park, a player who tended to keep his own counsel in a sometimes boisterous dressing room but who allowed his skills to speak eloquently on the pitch. The stocky Liverpudlian was a talented wing-half, quick of brain and sharp of tackle, whose neat control, precise distribution and powerful shot offered expert support to the Trotters' front line. Indeed, Johnny was pressed into occasional service as an emergency striker, never more devastatingly than at home to Blackpool in January 1953, when he plundered a hat-trick. On the debit side, his habit of surging forward from midfield at every opportunity sometimes left alarming defensive gaps, particularly in the latter stages of his Wanderers tenure. Johnny was Bill Ridding's first signing as Bolton boss, arriving from Tranmere - where Bill had been trainer - in February 1951. The promising 22-year-old went straight into the first team and he remained an automatic selection throughout the mid-1950s. He picked up an FA Cup Final loser's medal against Blackpool in 1953, putting the disappointment behind him the following year when he won his sole England cap, against Northern Ireland. That day at Windsor Park, Johnny eclipsed the superb creative skills of Jimmy McIlroy and could consider himself unlucky not to be given a second chance. In September 1956, despite his increased stature in the game, Bolton allowed the thoughtful Wheeler to join his cousin, Ron Moran, at Liverpool, where he stayed long enough to take part in the first stirrings of the Bill Shankly-inspired Red revolution. Johnny, who wasn't lacking in typical Scouse wit despite his preference for not shouting the odds, later became trainer and assistant manager at Bury.

strike partner, the dark-haired Scot Willie Moir, topped the First Division scoring chart with 25 goals in 1948/49.

Undeniably, though, fresh impetus was needed and it arrived in October 1950, facilitated rather poignantly by the retirement through ill health of the faithful Rowley. He was replaced by club trainer Bill Ridding, who had assisted with the

HAROLD HASSALL
1951/52 - 1954/55

As he prepared to face Chelsea at Burnden Park on New Year's Day 1955, Harold Hassall had everything to look forward to. A skilful, refined inside-forward with five England caps already to his name, he was only 25 and it seemed reasonable to suppose that his prime lay ahead. But then came calamity. That afternoon against the Pensioners he damaged his knee so badly that he never played again, leaving club and country to mourn what might have been. A Lancastrian who began his professional career in Yorkshire with Huddersfield, Harold was a current international when he joined Bolton for £27,000 in January 1952. He was bought to replace Willie Moir as a foil to Nat Lofthouse, and chipped in with some valuable goals, picking up crumbs from the great man's table. But Harold's forte was creating chances for others, his smooth control and imaginative distribution providing crucial balance in a Bolton side that was already long on muscle and effort. He was quick, too, and versatile, the last-mentioned quality being needed in the 1953 FA Cup Final against Blackpool, when he dropped back to wing-half after injury to Eric Bell necessitated a reshuffle. As it happened, that switch did not have the happiest of outcomes for the Trotters, Harold deflecting a shot from Stan Mortensen into his own net for the Seasiders' opening goal. However, only killjoys would have dreamed of depriving Stan of the first hat-trick in a Wembley final by entering 'Hassall og' on the scoresheet. After his enforced retirement, Harold turned to teaching, for which he was already qualified. Later he coached the England youth side, worked in sports administration and became secretary of the Amateur Swimming Association.

BANNISTER, Neville
Burnley, 21 July, 1937

Bolton W.	07.54	26	0	4
Lincoln C.	03.61	68	0	16
Hartlepool U.	08.64	41	0	8
Rochdale	07.65	18	1	2

BARNARD, Arthur
Mossley, 20 June, 1932

Bolton W.	11.51	2	0	0
Stockport Co.	07.56	53	0	0
Southport	09.59	42	0	0

BARNES, Peter Simon
Manchester, 10 June, 1957

Manchester C.	08.74	108	7	15
West Bromwich A.	07.79	76	1	23
Leeds U.	08.81	31	0	1
Leeds U.	08.83	25	2	4
Coventry C.	10.84	18	0	2
Manchester U.	07.85	19	1	2
Manchester C.	01.87	8	0	0
Bolton W.	10.87	2	0	0
Port Vale	12.87	3	0	0
Hull C.	03.88	11	0	0
Bolton W.	11.88	2	1	0
Sunderland	02.89	1	0	0

BARRASS, Malcolm Williamson
Blackpool, 13 December, 1924

Bolton W.	11.44	329	0	25
Sheffield U.	09.56	18	0	0

BEARDS, Alan
Normanton, 19 October, 1932

Bolton W.	10.50	14	0	2
Swindon T.	03.54	21	0	4
Stockport Co.	07.55	5	0	0

BEECH, Harry William
Kearsley, 7 January, 1946

Bolton W.	06.64	14	1	0
Stockport Co.	07.67	2	2	0

BELL, Eric
Manchester, 27 November, 1929

Bolton W.	11.49	102	0	1

BELL, Graham Thomas
Middleton, 30 March, 1955

Oldham Ath.	12.73	166	4	9
Preston N.E.	03.79	140	3	9
Huddersfield T.	11.81	2	0	0
Carlisle U.	08.83	11	3	0
Bolton W.	02.84	86	6	3
Tranmere Rov.	08.86	41	1	4

BENNETT, Michael
Bolton, 24 December, 1962

Bolton W.	01.80	62	3	1
Wolverhampton W.	06.83	6	0	0
Cambridge U.	03.84	76	0	0
Preston N.E.	09.86	85	1	1
Carlisle U.	08.90	21	3	0

BERRY, Neil
Edinburgh, 6 April, 1963

Bolton W.	03.81	25	7	0

preparation of the England team for that summer's World Cup Finals in Brazil. That might have been considered a dubious qualification, in view of England's humiliating exit from the tournament, but the Bolton board knew their man well, and before long their judgement was vindicated handsomely. At first only in temporary charge, the former tram conductor transformed a distinctly lacklustre team into one to be respected.

After consolidating with an eminently acceptable eighth-place finish in 1950/51, Bolton set the First Division pace the following term, losing only one of their first 11 matches. By now Bobby Langton, signed from Preston North End in 1949, was producing the type of displays that had made him an England winger, and further quality arrived in the form of Harold Hassall from Huddersfield Town for a club record £27,000 in January 1952.

But despite the blooding in October of richly talented inside-forward Ray Parry at the tender age of 15 years and 267 days, and the mid-season introduction of the promising Doug Holden at outside-right, results deteriorated as the campaign wore on. Eventually Ridding's men finished in fifth place, nine points behind champions Manchester United, but, such regrettable anti-climax notwithstanding, one of

---

BRYAN EDWARDS 1950/51 - 1964/65

It is almost impossible to exaggerate the influence of doughty Bryan Edwards on the post-war history of Bolton Wanderers. The cool, reliable Yorkshireman turned in fabulously consistent performances for a full decade and a half, and but for National Service he must have beaten the Trotters' appearance record, then held by between-the-wars left-back Alex Finney. Bryan was a defensive stalwart who spent the 1950s at left-half - apart from brief spells deputising for his friends, Tommy Banks and John Higgins, at left-back and centre-half respectively - and then switched to the number-five shirt when Higgins retired in 1960/61. Combative in the air and strong in the tackle, he was never ambitious on the ball, preferring to win it and then slip it to a colleague. In this mode he formed a productive partnership with Banks, who was more inclined towards imaginative distribution. As well as that record, Bryan's call-up cost him the chance of an appearance in the 1953 FA Cup Final against Blackpool, though he made up for it five years later, picking up a winner's medal against Manchester United. That day he made an early impact on proceedings, roving forward with uncharacteristic abandon after only three minutes to deliver a speculative pass which was deflected into the path of Nat Lofthouse, who duly opened the scoring. After his conversion to stopper, Bryan became the elder statesman of the side, his experience proving invaluable to young wing-halves Warwick Rimmer and Graham Stanley. After leaving Wanderers he coached at Blackpool, Preston and Plymouth, then managed Bradford City for three years before serving Huddersfield, Leeds and Bradford City again in a variety of roles, including physiotherapist.

the Wanderers' most productive eras was firmly under way.

Hopes had rarely been higher than at the start of 1952/53. Now Wanderers were a team of real attacking flair and dash; indeed, they could field an all-international forward line of Billy Hughes (Northern Ireland), Moir (Scotland), Lofthouse, Hassall and Langton (all England). Their Achilles heel, however, was a leaky rearguard whose lack of consistency made life difficult in the

First Division. Burnden Park witnessed a microcosm of Bolton's League season on Christmas Day when Lofthouse and Moir each netted twice against Arsenal, but the Gunners garnered the yuletide spoils by scoring six!

That left the Cup, which was to furnish royal entertainment and climax in the most heart-stopping Wembley finale of them all. As they progressed towards the Twin Towers, Bolton owed *so* much to Lofthouse, now

BINGLEY, Walter
Sheffield, 17 April, 1930

Bolton W.	04.48	6	0	0
Sheffield Wed.	05.55	38	0	0
Swindon T.	01.58	101	0	0
York C.	08.60	130	0	5
Halifax T.	07.63	63	0	1

BIRCH, Brian
Southport, 9 April, 1938

Bolton W.	04.55	165	0	23
Rochdale	07.64	60	1	6

BOLLANDS, John Frederick
Middlesbrough, 11 July, 1935

Oldham Ath.	05.53	23	0	0
Sunderland	03.56	61	0	0
Bolton W,	02.60	13	0	0
Oldham Ath.	09.61	131	0	0

BOOTH, Paul
Bolton, 7 December, 1965

Bolton W.	12.83	1	0	0
Crewe Alex.	07.85	23	4	0

BORROWS, Brian
Liverpool, 20 December, 1960

Everton	04.80	27	0	0
Bolton W.	03.83	95	0	0
Coventry C.	06.85	326	4	11
Bristol C.	09.93	6	0	0

BOSWELL, Alan Henry
Walsall, 8 August, 1943

Walsall	08.60	66	0	0
Shrewsbury T.	08.63	222	0	0
Wolverhampton W.	09.68	10	0	0
Bolton W.	10.69	51	0	0
Port Vale	08.72	86	0	0

BRADLEY, John (Jack)
Hemsworth, 27 November, 1916

Huddersfield T.	11.35			
Swindon T.	08.36	24	0	5
Chelsea	06.38			
Southampton	05.39	49	0	22
Bolton W.	10.47	92	0	19
Norwich C.	11.50	6	0	0

BRANAGAN Keith Graham
Fulham, 10 July, 1966

Cambridge U.	08.83	110	0	0
Millwall	03.88	46	0	0
Brentford	11.89	2	0	0
Gillingham	10.91	1	0	0
Bolton W.	07.92	56	0	0

BRENNAN, Ian
Easington, 25 March, 1953

Burnley	10.70	173	2	11
Bolton W.	12.80	16	1	0

BROMILOW, Geoffrey W.
Farnworth, 14 September, 1945

Bolton W. (Am)	10.6	3	2	0

BROMLEY, Brian
Burnley, 20 March, 1946

Bolton W.	03.63	165	1	25

enshsrined as 'The Lion of Vienna' and the regular leader of England's line. He scored in every round - hitting the target against Fulham in the third, Notts County in the fourth (in two out of three matches), Luton Town in the fifth and plucky little Gateshead in the sixth. Then he netted twice in a pulsating 4-3 semi-final victory over Everton at Maine Road, in which Bolton found themselves hanging on for dear life in the closing minutes after leading 4-0.

Small wonder, then, that come Cup Final week 'Lofty' was named Footballer of the Year, having scored eight times for England to cap a season of personal triumph. But could he add still further icing to an already heavily embellished cake by helping to take the English game's oldest senior trophy back to Burnden Park?

The answer, as every student of soccer history must know, came in the negative, though the Trotters' defeat by Lancastrian neighbours Blackpool was nothing if not glorious. Through no fault of their own, Bolton were cast as 'villains' of the piece by a public desperate to see Stanley Matthews, the 38-year-old Peter Pan of football, pocket a winner's medal at his third, and surely final, attempt.

However, fortified after every pre-Cup tie training session by their own special drink - concocted from two dozen eggs and two bottles of sherry - Lofthouse and company started the game at a gallop. After only two minutes, the bustling spearhead gave his side

TOMMY BANKS 1947/48 - 1960/61

Lurid tales of cinder tracks and hapless wingers being forcibly deposited on to or over them tell only part of the story of Tommy Banks. Of course, the ebullient little Lancastrian left-back was a hard man, and there were times - plenty of them! - when he used his muscle to bruising effect. But no one should doubt the rarely emphasised fact that Tommy was a fine all-round footballer. Unlike many defenders of his day, he could control the ball with ease and dispatch it accurately with either foot; he was quick, too, and would have prospered as an overlapper in the modern era. Tommy, whose older brother Ralph also served Bolton long and well as a full-back, was an outstanding youth player who represented the Boys Clubs of Great Britain and England. He attracted interest from the likes of Wolves, Manchester United, Leeds and Portsmouth before signing on at Burnden Park, winning a regular first-team place in 1953/54 and retaining it until 1960. Tommy had reached his peak in 1958, when he won the first of his six England caps during the World Cup Finals in Sweden and was the subject of a discreet inquiry by Manchester United, rebuilding in the aftermath of the Munich air disaster. However, Bolton didn't want to sell and the former pitman remained a Trotter until a series of muscle injuries curtailed his top-class career. In 1961 he joined non-League Altrincham before throwing himself with typical wholeheartedness into the building trade in his home town of Farnworth. In his mid-sixties, he was fitter and stronger than many men half his age. Then, as in his playing heyday, Tommy Banks was a formidable character.

Portsmouth	11.68	88	1	3
Brighton & H.A.	11.71	47	3	3
Reading	T09.73	13	1	2
Darlington	02.75	3	0	0

BROOKMAN, Nicholas Anthony
Manchester, 28 October, 1968

Bolton W.	11.86	47	10	10
Stockport Co.	03.90	4	2	0

BROWN, Michael Anthony
Birmingham, 8 February, 1968

Shrewsbury T.	02.86	174	16	9
Bolton W.	08.91	27	6	3
Shrewsbury T.	12.92	6	0	1
Shrewsbury T.	03.93	51	1	7

BROWN, Philip
South Shields, 30 May, 1959

Hartlepool U.	07.78	210	7	8
Halifax T.	07.85	135	0	19
Bolton W.	06.88	254	2	14

BURGESS, Arthur Campbell (Cam)
Birkenhead, 21 September, 1919

Bolton W.	02.38	5	0	3
Chester C.	10.48	111	0	64
Crystal Palace	09.51	47	0	40
York C.	07.53	32	0	14

BURKE, David Ian
Liverpool, 6 August, 1960

Bolton W.	08.77	65	4	1
Huddersfield T.	06.81	189	0	3
Crystal Palace	10.87	80	1	0
Bolton W.	07.90	104	2	0

BUTLER, Dennis Anthony
Macclesfield, 24 April, 1944

Bolton W.	06.61	62	3	11
Rochdale	02.68	152	4	34

BYROM, John
Blackburn, 28 July, 1944

Blackburn Rov.	08.61	106	2	45
Bolton W.	06.66	296	8	113
Blackburn Rov.	09.76	15	1	5

CALDWELL, Anthony
Salford, 21 March, 1958

Bolton W.	06.83	131	8	58
Bristol C.	07.87	9	8	3
Chester C.	01.88	4	0	0
Grimsby T.	09.88	2	1	0
Stockport Co.	10.88	23	3	6

CALLAGHAN, Ian Michael
Prescot, 5 August, 1969

Bolton W.	07.87	1	0	0

CAME, Mark Raymond
Exeter, 14 September, 1961

Bolton W.	04.84	188	7	7
Chester C.	12.92	47	0	1

CANTELLO, Leonard
Manchester, 11 September, 1951

West Bromwich A.	10.68	297	4	13

the lead with an underhit shot from just outside the area which deceived Seasiders 'keeper George Farm. Thus inspired, Bolton comtinued to pour forward even after a

hamstring strain reduced left-half Eric Bell to a passenger on the wing, and Lofthouse came close to doubling the lead, only to see his shot bounce back off a post.

RAY PARRY 1951/52 - 1960/61

Ray Parry was a 'golden boy' of the 1950s who was said to possess only one foot, his left, but that one was worth three! He went on to enjoy an eminently worthy career with three Lancashire clubs, yet without scaling the expected heights. There had seemed no limits to his horizons in October 1951 when he made his Wanderers debut at home to Wolves, becoming the youngest player in First Division history at 15 years and 267 days. That term the precocious, Derby-born inside-forward was given only two outings, but was a more familiar face in 1952/53 before becoming fully established - briefly on the left wing, then in his favoured number-ten shirt - for the remainder of the decade. By the late 1950s, experienced yet still in his early twenties, Ray had matured into a classy performer who could pass with the accuracy and subtlety of a schemer and strike with the venom of a spearhead. Indeed, his power of shot was compared to that of Bobby Charlton, and he used it to devastating effect from a free-kick in the 1958 FA Cup quarter-final victory over Wolves. That season Ray picked up a Wembley winner's medal, in 1959 he won the first of his two full caps; surely the path to stardom was stretching before him. Some reckoned he needed a move to one of the biggest clubs to realise his potential but instead, in October 1960, a £25,000 fee took him to Blackpool, who were of similar stature to the Trotters. Ray served the Seasiders for four years, but his form hit a plateau, acceptable enough but not living up to earlier hints of true excellence. He went on to give Bury seven seasons, thus completing a 20-year professional career. Ray, whose brothers Jack and Cyril played for Derby and Notts County respectively, is still a much-loved figure in Bolton, where he was a newsagent during the 1970s and 1980s.

Bolton W.	06.79	89	1	3
Hereford U. (N/C)	01.83	1	0	0
Bury (N/C)	02.83	8	1	1

CARTER, Michael
Warrington, 18 April, 1960
Bolton W.	07.77	37	12	8
Mansfield T.	03.79	18	0	4
Swindon T.	03.82	4	1	0
Plymouth Arg.	08.82	6	6	1
Hereford U.	03.83	91	6	11
Wrexham	07.87	25	9	7

CHANDLER, Jeffrey George
Hammersmith, 19 June, 1959
Blackpool	08.76	31	6	7
Leeds U.	09.79	21	5	2
Bolton W.	10.81	152	5	36
Derby Co.	07.85	45	1	9
Mansfield T.	11.86	6	0	0
Bolton W.	07.87	18	6	4
Cardiff C.	11.89	21	4	1

CHARNLEY, James (Chic)
Glasgow, 11 June, 1963
Bolton W. (L)	03.92	3	0	0

CLARKE, Peter A.
Bolton, 6 July, 1949
Bolton W.	06.69	13	0	0
Stockport Co.	07.71	49	0	0

CLEMENT, David Thomas
Battersea, 2 February, 1948   Died 1982
Queens Park R.	07.65	402	3	22
Bolton W.	06.79	33	0	0
Fulham	10.80	17	1	0
Wimbledon	10.81	9	0	2

CLEMENTS, Andrew Paul
Swindon, 11 October, 1955
Bolton W.	10.73	1	0	0
Port Vale	02.77	2	1	0
York C.	11.77	146	2	6

CODD, Ronald William
Sheffield, 3 December, 1928
Bolton W.	03.50	31	0	5
Sheffield Wed.	03.53	2	0	0
Barrow	10.54	45	0	11

COMSTIVE, Paul Thomas
Southport, 25 November, 1961
Blackburn Rov.	10.79	3	3	0
Rochdale	09.82	9	0	2
Wigan Ath.	08.83	35	0	2
Wrexham	11.84	95	4	8
Burnley	08.87	81	1	17
Bolton W.	09.89	42	7	3
Chester C.	11.91	55	2	6

COOPER, Charles
Farnworth, 14 June, 1941
Bolton W.	05.59	79	4	0
Barrow	07.69	54	0	0

CORFIELD, Ernest
Wigan, 18 January, 1931
Bolton W.	04.48	6	0	0
Stockport Co.	07.53	2	0	0

29

Stan Mortensen equalised on 35 minutes, but Bolton were back in front by the interval, Moir being credited with a glancing header from Langton's cross, although television replays suggest he may not have made contact. After the break the Trotters' momentum continued, and when the stricken Bell jumped off his good leg to nod his side to a 3-1 advantage, the destination of the Cup seemed settled.

But with half an hour left, Matthews took over. Running riot on the left flank of the Bolton defence - in which full-back Ralph Banks had now joined Bell among the ranks of the injured - Stanley sparked a Blackpool resurgence that brought Mortensen goals in the 68th and 89th minutes, then created the winner for Bill Perry two minutes into injury time.

So the Cup had been dashed from the Trotters' lips in the cruellest fashion, but even in that moment of despair, Lofthouse found the spirit to applaud his conquerors' winning strike, the true mark of an exceptional sportsman.

If only Bolton had reorganised their back line when two goals up, and opted to soak up pressure instead of retaining their attacking

Lofthouse gets in his shot despite the close attentions of Blackpool's Harry Johnston and Tom Garret.

formation, the outcome might have been different. But that was not their way, and they will be remembered as the most valiant and honourable of Wembley losers.

That Wanderers side, whose names are emblazoned forever in the annals of the club, lined up like this: Stan Hanson in goal, full-backs John Ball and Ralph Banks; a half-back trio of Johnny Wheeler, Malcolm Barrass and Eric Bell; and a front line of Doug Holden, Willie Moir, Nat Lofthouse, Harold Hassall and Bobby Langton. For nine of them, the chance of Cup Final glory had gone forever; but for Holden and Lofthouse, Dame Fortune had a happier fate in store.

Top: Hanson clears his lines as Blackpool exert heavy pressure.

Centre: Moir beats Farm to restore Bolton's lead.

Bottom: The stricken Bell rises to nod the Trotters' third goal.

31

DOUG HOLDEN
1951/52 - 1962/63

No one in his right senses would compare Doug Holden to the two great wingers of his era - clearly Messrs Matthews and Finney were well out of reach of mere mortals - but the blond Mancunian *does* qualify as one of the very best of the rest. Capable of playing on either flank - most of his Bolton career was spent on the right, with a four-season spell on the left around the turn of the decade - he was blessed with magnetic control, the knack of tricking his way past defenders and a splendid awareness of passing options around him. Doug wasn't the quickest of wingmen but he was one of the most industrious, ever-ready to chase back and help in defence, and he would have been ideally suited to the modern game. Many Lofthouse goals emanated from perfectly-flighted Holden crosses and while he was not prolific himself - only once, in 1961/62, did his tally reach double figures - his high number of 'assists' made that irrelevant. One of his finest performances came in the 1953 FA Cup Final, a fact not widely reported as all the plaudits that day went to the aforementioned Mr M. Nevertheless, Doug had his day, returning to Wembley in 1958 to pocket a deserved winner's medal. He was back again six years later, too, opening the scoring against West Ham for Preston, whom he had joined in November 1962. In retrospect, the decision to release Doug, who had won five England caps in 1959, was premature. Bolton could have done with his experience as they struggled to stay in the First Division but decided that, as he was 32, his day was probably done. After three terms at Deepdale, Doug played and coached in Australia before coming back to England to train Grimsby.

COWDRILL, Barry James
Birmingham, 3 January, 1957

West Bromwich A.	04.79	127	4	0
Rotherham U.	10.85	2	0	0
Bolton W.	07.88	117	2	4
Rochdale	02.92	15	0	1

COYLE, Owen Columba
Glasgow, 14 July, 1966

Bolton W.	07.93	25	3	7

CROMBIE, Dean Malcolm
Lincoln, 9 August, 1957

Lincoln C.	02.77	33	0	0
Grimsby T.	08.78	316	4	3
Reading	11.86	4	0	0
Bolton W.	08.87	90	5	1
Lincoln C.	01.91	0	1	0

CROOK, Walter
Chorley, 28 April, 1913   Died 1988

Blackburn Rov.	01.31	218	0	2
Bolton W.	05.47	28	0	0

CROSS, David
Heywood, 8 December, 1950

Rochdale	08.69	50	9	21
Norwich C.	10.71	83	1	21
Coventry C.	11.73	90	1	30
West Bromwich A.	11.76	38	0	18
West Ham U.	12.77	178	1	77
Manchester C.	08.82	31	0	12
Oldham Ath.	10.83	18	4	6
West Bromwich A.	10.84	16	0	2
Bolton W.	06.85	19	1	8
Bury	01.86	12	1	0

CUNLIFFE, James Graham
Hindley, 16 June, 1936

Bolton W.	01.55	25	0	0
Rochdale	07.64	36	0	0

CUNNINGHAM, Anthony E.
Jamaica, 12 November, 1957

Lincoln C.	05.79	111	12	32
Barnsley	09.82	40	2	11
Sheffield Wed.	11.83	26	2	5
Manchester C.	07.84	16	2	1
Newcastle U.	02.85	37	10	4
Blackpool	08.87	71	0	17
Bury	08.89	55	3	17
Bolton W.	03.91	9	0	4
Rotherham U.	08.91	65	4	24
Doncaster Rov.	07.93	19	6	1
Wycombe W.	03.94	4	1	0

CURRAN, Hugh Patrick
Glasgow, 25 September, 1943

Millwall	03.64	57	0	26
Norwich C.	01.66	112	0	46
Wolverhampton W.	01.69	77	5	40
Oxford U.	09.72	69	1	28
Bolton W.	09.74	40	7	13
Oxford U.	07.77	30	5	11

DARBY, Julian Timothy
Bolton, 3 October, 1967

Bolton W.	07.86	258	12	36
Coventry C.	10.93	25	1	5

Disappointed but undismayed by this debilitating reverse, Bolton reacted positively by mounting a concerted challenge for both League and Cup in 1953/54. They finished fifth in the First Division, nine points adrift of top dogs Wolves, and their knockout bandwagon reached the quarter-final stage, where it was halted by Sheffield Wednesday.

By this time it had become apparent to the shrewd Ridding that if Wanderers were to have realistic hopes of winning a major prize, then a radical team reconstruction job was in order. Without bottomless coffers to draw on, he placed his faith in youth and while the senior side marked time - finishing eighteenth, eighth and ninth in the table over the next three seasons - the youngsters began to suggest that his confidence in them had not been misplaced.

In 1954/55 the reserves won the Central League title for the first and only time in the club's history and a year later Ridding's rookies reached the semi-final of the FA Youth Cup. Gradually they filtered through into the first team and the 1956/57 League double over the champions, the Busby Babes of Manchester United, spoke volumes for their progress.

Season 1957/58 saw the first floodlit match at Burnden Park, a drawn friendly against Heart of Midlothian, but more momentous events

ROY HARTLE 1952/53 - 1965/66

Roy Hartle was something of a legend, not just in Bolton but throughout English football. The tall, curly-haired right-back was branded the archetypal hard man by opposing fans, the type who tears wingers limb from limb and then spits out the bones. Now, it would be idle to contend that Roy's lurid image was built entirely on fantasy. After all, he was fearsomely strong in the tackle, he could kick like a mule and few forwards relished a close encounter with the muscular Midlander. But, in truth, he was no tougher than his team-mates, nor any number of combative operators at other top clubs and it would be unfair if that reputation were to obscure considerable all-round capabilities, especially his keen positional sense. Particularly when he played behind attacking wing-halves such as Johnny Wheeler or Derek Hennin, often he was left exposed at the back and needed to read the game shrewdly to protect his flank - and he did so to great effect. Roy made his Wanderers debut in 1952/53 and impressed, but after playing in every FA Cup round was devastated when dropped for the final in favour of John Ball. However, after completing his National Service alongside full-back partner Tommy Banks, he returned in 1955 to claim a regular place for the next 11 seasons, the highlight of that sequence being the FA Cup triumph over Manchester United in 1958. Few wingers, including the incomparable Tom Finney, got the better of Bolton's craggy number two, though one who troubled him more than most was Derek Hogg in his Leicester and West Bromwich days. Roy, a quiet, well-spoken individual, left Burnden in 1966, after which he coached in America and scouted for Bury, then managed a brewery.

JOHN HIGGINS 1952/53 - 1960/61

When introducing new Liverpool signing Ron Yeats to reporters, a gleeful Bill Shankly rasped: 'Take a walk around my centre-half, gentlemen.' Had he been blessed with an equally colourful turn of phrase, Bolton boss Bill Ridding might have said much the same of John Higgins, the colossus at the core of Wanderers' famous 1950s rearguard. Weighing more than 14 stone and standing 6ft-plus, John presented a formidable barrier at a time when big, bustling centre-forwards were very much in vogue. Sparks flew when he went into battle against the likes of Bobby Smith, Derek Kevan or Dave Hickson, yet although strength in both aerial and ground combat was a prominent component of the Higgins game, by no means was he a mere bruiser. While perhaps not as deft in possession as Malcolm Barrass, the man whose regular place he took in 1956/57, John could use the ball accurately enough and sometimes he surprised supporters with a gem of a pass. He joined the Trotters as a full-back in 1950, but as he grew to his full bulk it became apparent that centre-half was his natural berth. John was at his zenith in 1957/58, when he was vice-captain and didn't miss a game in League or FA Cup. He performed immaculately at Wembley against Manchester United, and there were those who believed he could not have been far away from the England reckoning. That call never came, but he continued as Bolton's first-choice pivot until mid-1960/61, when he had slowed down, and wing-half Bryan Edwards shifted to the middle. John - whose son Mark (also a centre-half) captained Everton and recovered from serious injury to serve Manchester United, Bury and Stoke - saw out his playing days in the non-League ranks. In the late 1980s he was general manager of Stockport.

DARLING, Malcolm
Arbroath, 4 July, 1947

Blackburn Rov.	10.64	114	14	30
Norwich C.	05.70	16	0	5
Rochdale	10.71	82	4	16
Bolton W.	09.73	6	2	0
Chesterfield	08.74	100	4	33
Stockport Co.	03.77	11	0	2
Sheffield Wed.	08.77	1	1	0
Hartlepool U.	09.77	2	2	0
Bury (N/C)	03.78	1	1	0

DAVIES, Ronald Wyn
Caernarfon, 20 March, 1942

Wrexham	04.60	55	0	22
Bolton W.	03.62	155	0	66
Newcastle U.	10.66	181	0	40
Manchester C.	08.71	45	0	8
Manchester U.	09.72	15	1	4
Blackpool	06.73	34	2	5
Crystal Palace	08.74	3	0	0
Stockport Co.	08.75	28	2	7
Crewe Alex.	08.76	50	5	13

DAVISON, Aidan John
Sedgefield, 11 May, 1968

Notts Co.	03.88	1	0	0
Bury	10.89			
Millwall	08.91	34	0	0
Bolton W.	07.93	30	1	0

DAVISON, James Hawkins
Sunderland, 1 November, 1942

Sunderland	11.59	62	0	10
Bolton W.	11.63	21	0	1

DEAKIN, Peter
Normanton, 25 March, 1938

Bolton W.	05.55	63	0	13
Peterborough U.	06.64	74	1	34
Bradford P.A.	09.66	36	0	9
Peterborough U.	09.67	16	0	1
Brentford	07.68	7	1	2

DEAKIN, Raymond John
Liverpool, 19 June, 1959

Everton	06.77			
Port Vale	08.81	21	2	6
Bolton W.	08.82	104	1	2
Burnley	07.85	212	1	6

DEAN, Joseph
Manchester, 4 April, 1939

Bolton W.	04.56	17	0	0
Carlisle U.	07.62	137	0	0
Barrow	07.70	41	0	0

DENTON, Roger W.
Stretford, 6 January, 1953

Bolton W.	05.71	3	1	0
Bradford C.	07.72	25	5	0
Rochdale	02.74	2	0	0

DIBBLE, Andrew Gerald
Cwmbran, 8 May, 1965

Cardiff C.	08.82	62	0	0
Luton T.	07.84	30	0	0
Sunderland	02.86	12	0	0

were in store. True, Bolton suffered a poor League campaign, dropping back to 15th and securing only six more points than relegated Sunderland, but the FA Cup produced a dramatically different story.

This time the campaign began at Deepdale, the home of local rivals Preston, then challenging for the Championship. Given precious little chance against an in-form Tom Finney and company, the Trotters rose magnificently to the occasion, winning 3-0 thanks to a brace of goals from Ray Parry and one from young Dennis Stevens. The fourth round brought unexpectedly dogged resistance from courageous York City, who earned a goalless draw at Bootham Crescent before capitulating 3-0 at Burnden, with the injured Lofthouse's understudy, Terry Allcock, striking twice and winger Brian Birch once.

Next came a 3-1 home triumph over Stoke City (with Lofthouse, Parry and Stevens on target) to set up what proved to be

DEREK HENNIN
1953/54 - 1960/61

Derek Hennin was a veritable dreadnought of a footballer. Even in a team that prided itself on its strength and fitness, the affable Merseysider stood out for his non-stop effort and magnificent athleticism, running tirelessly, tackling ferociously, almost robotic in his refusal to submit to fatigue. In truth, this physical dimension to Derek's game was all-important because he was never the most naturally gifted of players. His customary position was right-half, and though he could be doughty in defence, there was nothing he loved better than charging forward to attack. At times, this saddled right-back Roy Hartle with extra responsibilities, but the pair worked well together and Derek could set off on his buccaneering excursions knowing that precious little got past Roy. England youth international Hennin turned professional with Bolton in 1949, but did not make his senior debut until spring 1954, when an injury to Johnny Wheeler pitched him into a title race over the season's final quarter. Derek let no one down, but it was not till Johnny joined Liverpool in 1956 that the younger man claimed a regular place. He picked up an FA Cup winner's medal in 1958, and remained first choice until the emergence of Graham Stanley in 1960. Derek, who died in 1987, completed his career at Chester. During the second half of the 1950s, his value to Bolton had been enhanced by stints as an emergency centre-forward, his finest hour coming in April 1958 when he plundered a hat-trick at home to Aston Villa. Another fond memory concerns the Burnden clash with Sheffield Wednesday some 13 months earlier, when Derek shot, the 'keeper caught cleanly, only for Nat Lofthouse to barge man and ball over the line for a goal. Sound familiar?

a memorable meeting with League leaders Wolves at Burnden Park. Bolton were reduced to ten fit men after right-half Derek Hennin suffered a muscle strain early in

proceedings, yet managed to snatch the lead through Stevens. But when Wolves regained parity two minutes later through Bobby Mason, the likelihood was that the

Cup favourites would seize the upper hand. The Trotters had not read that particular script, however, and Parry restored their lead with a 55th-minute free-kick. Now Wolves roared forward and laid siege to the Bolton goal, putting England custodian Eddie Hopkinson and his defenders under ceaseless pressure. Heroically they survived to the 80th minute, only to receive a hammer- blow as Parry was concussed in a collision and carried off. Thus reduced to nine men sound in wind and limb, with the dauntless Hennin able to offer little more than nuisance value, they soldiered on, and when the final whistle signalled their gallant victory, the roar from the 56,000-plus crowd might have been heard all over Lancashire.

Having disposed of the two best teams in the First Division, Bolton now faced one of the finest in the Second, soon-to-be-promoted Blackburn Rovers, in the semi-final at Maine Road. For this Red Rose derby, they were deprived once more of Lofthouse, who had damaged a shoulder, but all was well as his deputy, reserve winger Ralph Gubbins, grabbed both goals in a 2-1 win for the Wanderers.

Having led Bolton to Wembley for the second

DENNIS STEVENS
1953/54 - 1961/62

Dennis Stevens was a study in perpetual motion, a teak-tough, tireless inside-forward who sped around the pitch, chasing, tackling and shooting as if his life depended on it. The chunky Midlander - a cousin of Manchester United's incomparable Duncan Edwards - was not short of skill, but it was his vigour which made the most indelible impression on opponents. Indeed, as one of his 1950s team-mates recalled affectionately: 'They used to queue up to clobber Stevie - but they had to catch him first!' Dennis made his senior debut in autumn 1953, becoming a regular in 1955/56 after injury had forced Harold Hassall to quit. He continued to make steady progress, netting 13 League goals in each of four consecutive seasons as well as creating plenty for Nat Lofthouse and company. His prowess was recognised with selection for both the Football League and England under-23s, though a full cap continued to elude him, even after he was called into Walter Winterbottom's squad in 1957. Dennis gave a typically bouncy display in the 1958 FA Cup Final - it was his powerful shot which resulted in Nat's controversial second goal - and he did his reputation no harm when he netted 15 times as stand-in centre-forward when the great man was sidelined in 1959/60. Dennis continued to delight the Burnden regulars until March 1962 when Everton, eager for his irrepressible input, secured his services for £35,000. Many Trotters' fans complained that the fee was outrageously low and they were proved right as Dennis, playing in a deeper role at Goodison, became a crucial member of the Blues' 1963 Championship side. Eventually he moved on to Oldham, then Tranmere, whom he assisted on their rise from the Fourth Division, before injury forced him into retirement and the clothes business.

time in five years, no praise should have been too high for Ridding, especially as his side cost only £110, each member having set the club back no more than a £10 signing-on fee. Yet for the second time, the Burnden Park outfit found themselves playing distinctly second fiddle to their opponents in the pre-match publicity. In 1953 Stanley Matthews had monopolised the headlines and the neutrals' sympathy; now it was Manchester United, who had performed something of a miracle in reaching the final only three months after the Munich air disaster.

Eight players had died and several more had been seriously injured when their plane had crashed on their way home from a European tie. Manager Matt Busby had narrowly escaped death and was not yet back at his desk, and the achievement of his assistant, Jimmy Murphy, in leading the patched-up Red Devils to Wembley well-nigh beggared belief.

Nevertheless, none of this was Bolton's fault, and it was hard, indeed, for them to be handed what amounted to another supporting role on soccer's gala day. In the circumstances, they deserve huge credit for disregarding the often-hysterical media build-up to the game, and getting on with the job in hand.

The men handed the responsibility for winning Wanderers' first major honour since the Cup was last claimed in 1929 were

BRIAN BIRCH
1954/55 - 1963/64

Brian Birch flattered to deceive. Not always, of course - there were days when the little-dark-haired flankman was utterly devastating - but often enough to limit his top-flight career to a handful of seasons as an almost-regular. Having made his senior debut as a 16-year-old in the autumn of 1954, Brian was tipped for stardom. After three seasons of consolidation, with considerably more Central League than first-team appearances, he appeared to come of age in 1957/58. That term he missed only a handful of League outings and was an FA Cup ever-present as the Trotters went all the way to Wembley, where they beat Manchester United. Still only 20, and with that coveted medal in his trophy cabinet, Brian seemed to have the soccer world at his feet. At his most effective on the right though capable of patrolling either touchline, he was a splendid crosser and direct runner who was ever willing to chase back and challenge for the ball if he lost possession. The diminutive Lancastrian packed a fierce shot, too, though he never scored heavily and his goals tended to come in clusters, presumably during periods when his confidence was high. He was, alas, inconsistent in the manner of so many wingers and in 1961 the arrival of Brian Pilkington from Burnley saw Doug Holden switch to the right, leaving the disappointed Birch as an occasional participant. He remained on the fringes until the summer of 1964 when he made the short trip to Rochdale. By then the momentum of Brian's career was gone and two campaigns for the Dale were followed by departure to the non-League scene.

goalkeeper Hopkinson, full-backs Roy Hartle and Tommy Banks (younger brother of Ralph), a half-back line of Hennin, John Higgins and Bryan Edwards, and forwards Birch, Stevens, skipper Lofthouse, Parry and Holden. While the attack retained a reputation for verve and vigour, Bolton were now renowned also for the uncompromising approach of the defence, in which the tackling of Hartle, Banks, Hennin

Huddersfield T.	03.87	5	0	0
Manchester C.	07.88	86	1	0
Middlesbrough	02.91	19	0	0
Bolton W.	09.91	13	0	0
West Bromwich A.	02.92	9	0	0

DILLON, Vincent
Manchester, 2 October, 1923

Bolton W.	04.48	17	0	2
Tranmere Rov.	02.51	33	0	17

DOBSON, John Martin
Blackburn, 14 February, 1948

Bolton W.	07.66			
Burnley	08.67	220	4	43
Everton	08.74	190	0	29
Burnley	08.79	186	0	20
Bury	03.84	60	1	4

DOYLE, Michael
Manchester, 25 November, 1946

Manchester C.	05.64	441	7	32
Stoke C.	06.78	115	0	5
Bolton W.	01.82	40	0	2
Rochdale	08.83	24	0	1

DUFFEY, Christopher Paul
Kirkby, 8 January, 1952

Bolton W.	09.69	8	0	0
Crewe Alex.	09.72	6	0	3
Crewe Alex.	07.73	54	3	12
Bury	10.74	17	4	8
Shrewsbury T.	05.75	4	4	1
Rochdale	11.75	2	0	0

DUNNE, Anthony Peter
Dublin, 24 July, 1941

Manchester U.	04.60	414	0	2
Bolton W.	08.73	166	4	0

EDISBURY, William
Tyldesley, 12 November, 1937

Bolton W.	10.56	2	0	0

EDWARDS, George Bryan
Leeds, 27 October, 1930

Bolton W.	10.47	482	0	8

EDWARDS, Jeffrey Gordon
Wrexham, 14 October, 1935

Bolton W.	10.52	3	0	0

EDWARDS, Malcolm
Wrexham, 25 October, 1939

Bolton W.	11.56	14	0	1
Chester C.	02.61	43	0	5
Tranmere Rov.	07.62	34	0	2
Barrow	07.64	177	0	9

ELLIOTT, Stephen Blair
Haltwhistle, 15 September, 1958

Nottingham F.	09.76	4	0	0
Preston N.E.	03.79	202	6	70
Luton T.	07.84	12	0	3
Walsall	12.84	68	1	21
Bolton W.	07.86	57	3	11
Bury	09.88	31	0	11
Rochdale	10.89	46	6	9

and Higgins was especially abrasive.

On paper, with United forced to field a fairly inexperienced and still partly traumatised side, the odds favoured the Trotters. Yet 'Murphy's Marvels' had come so far on fervour and the odd slice of fortune, and who was to say they would not carry on to a fairytale ending?

Nat Lofthouse, that's who. After only three minutes, he was on hand to net comfortably from five yards after Edwards' rather speculative pass was deflected into his path. After that, Bolton always looked the stronger, more ruthless unit, though they were given two frights by Munich survivor Bobby Charlton, one either side of the interval. First the

blond north-easterner shot ferociously to bring an athletic save from Hopkinson; then, with the 'keeper beaten, he cannoned another scorching drive against the inside of a post.

Almost immediately after that, Bolton gained

EDDIE HOPKINSON
1956/57 - 1969/70

Eddie Hopkinson occupies a special place in the folklore of Bolton Wanderers. Not only does he hold the club's appearance record with 578 senior outings between 1956 and 1969, he was also, and he remains, the best goalkeeper the Trotters have ever had. Though small for a custodian at 5ft 9in, the thickset north-easterner radiated confidence behind that formidable late-1950s rearguard. His agility and bravery in combination with an instinctive positional sense and a pair of seemingly prehensile hands more than made up for his lack of inches. Eddie excelled at every facet of the 'keeper's art, but his speciality was dealing with one-on-one situations. As a forward bore down on him, he would stand up until the last possible moment, then spread himself as the shot was released or his opponent attempted to jink past him - and it was extremely rare that he conceded a goal in such confrontations. Eddie, who made three amateur appearances for Oldham before signing for Bolton in November 1952, had to wait in line behind Stan Hanson and Ken Grieves for a first-team opportunity. It came in 1956 after Stan had retired and Ken was otherwise engaged on cricketing duty with Lancashire, and how 'Hoppy' made the most of it! He didn't miss a match that term and, surviving numerous attempts to dethrone him by good goalkeepers such as Joe Dean, Johnny Bollands and Alex Smith, he kept his job for nearly 14 seasons before yielding to Alan Boswell in November 1969. During that time Eddie's expertise had been rewarded with 14 England caps, won between 1957 and 1959, and he had known the joy of FA Cup Final victory in 1958. On the down side, he had spent the last six years of his tenure, while still an outstanding performer, in the Second Division, but there never seemed to be any question of such a loyal fellow asking to leave. After retiring as a player, Eddie coached the Wanderers' youngsters, had a spell as Stockport's assistant boss, then returned to Burnden as goalkeeping coach before leaving the game.

CONTROVERSIAL

Top: Lofthouse opens the scoring in the third minute. Below; the moment of impact as Nat barges Gregg, and the ball, over the line.

Irishman gathered the ball, Lofthouse barged into him with all his considerable might. 'Keeper and ball were deposited unceremoniously into the net and, unbelievably by today's standards, the referee signalled a goal.

Even at a time when net-minders were considered fair game for a brisk shoulder-to-shoulder challenge, many neutral observers believed it was an obvious foul. Meanwhile the Reds' fans were outraged, the Bolton contingent exultant - now the game was as good as over.

After receiving treatment in the net, the grounded Gregg was able to continue, and for a short period there was an extra bite to some of the Manchester tackling. But tempers cooled and the remaining 35 minutes passed without significant incident. Then, after collecting the Cup from Prince Philip, Lofthouse shared a drink with the fiery Gregg and - contrary to

a decisive lead, but their second goal was to be one of the most controversial in Cup Final history. It stemmed from the

workaholic Stevens, who cracked in a shot that United goalkeeper Harry Gregg could only push vertically into the air; as the red-haired

SUCCESS IN 1958

certain rumours - the two have remained the

Bill Ridding congratulates captain Lofthouse after the final whistlle.

best of friends ever since. Indeed, as the years passed, Harry turned the Lofthouse charge into a highlight of his after-dinner speaking routine, giving his version of events with a lurid twinkle in his eye but never with malice.

Back at Wembley on that sunny May afternoon, the most poignant moment came

when Matt Busby, still in pain from his awful injuries and leaning on a walking stick, arrived in the Trotters' dressing room to congratulate the victors. After shaking the hand of each player, he limped out through the door leaving Tommy Banks to remark to his hushed team-mates: 'That's the finest sportsman you'll ever see.'

Celebrating, left to right, are: Birch, Parry, Stevens, Holden, Hopkinson, Lofthouse, Higgins, Hennin, Hartle and Edwards.

47

Having tasted success with a young side, many of whom were barely in their prime - only 32-year-old Lofthouse was beyond his twenties - Bolton were at a crossroads. Would they forge ahead and consolidate as a major force, or would the Cup prove an isolated triumph?

They began 1958/59 in determined fashion, latching on to the leading group in the First Division and receiving the October boost of thrashing title-holders Wolves 4-1 in the Charity Shield at Burnden Park. Even though, come spring, it was the men from Molineux who were sitting pretty at the top of the table, Bolton could be reasonably content with their fourth place - only one lower than their best ever position, achieved in 1892, 1921 and 1925. They reached the Cup quarter-final, too,

FREDDIE HILL 1957/58 - 1968/69

Mention Freddie Hill to an average Bolton supporter of the 1960s and you need time to spare. The extravagantly gifted schemer was a favourite of the Burnden Park faithful throughout that decade - he remains, arguably, the most popular Trotter since Lofthouse himself - and the memories of his footballing wit and invention pour forth. Freddie's fans recall how he would 'kill' a ball with a single touch, then instantly dispatch a dagger-like pass through the heart of the opposing defence; or how he would shuffle past challenges with that deceptively graceless, stooping gait; or how, when a lay-off seemed the likely option, he might shoot, suddenly and explosively, to deadly effect. Sometimes when he left the pitch he was wearing the only clean pair of shorts on view, but so what? Freddie Hill wasn't a man to stop other people playing; he was out there to play himself, and that was what mattered. Sheffield-born, he spurned the Wednesday to join Bolton in 1957 and made his senior debut, aged 18, in April 1958. A long-term berth at inside-forward materialised in 1959/60 when Dennis Stevens moved to centre-forward to replace Lofthouse, and Freddie remained the brains of the Burnden Park attack until 1969. He played for England twice in 1962, and might have won more caps had his talents been paraded on a more glamorous stage. He asked for a move on several occasions, but seemed fated to stay at Burnden. The closest he came to getting away during his prime was when Liverpool, who saw him as an ideal replacement for Jimmy Melia, agreed a £60,000 fee only for the deal to fall through when Freddie failed a medical through high blood pressure, presumably brought on by all the excitement. When he did depart, eventually, it was in more prosaic circumstances, to Halifax for £5,000 in 1969, though later he had a brief taste of the big time with Manchester City, where he linked up once more with Francis Lee and Wyn Davies. Freddie's final League club was Peterborough, whom he left in 1974 to sample life in non-League circles. He continues to be regarded with affection at Burnden, where he had a testimonial match in 1991. Former team-mates recall still how they could give him the ball and take a rest while he bewildered the opposition; the fans revere him for producing a touch of magic. It's not a bad way to be remembered.

ELVY, Reginald
Leeds, 25 November, 1920   Died 1991

Halifax T.	03.44	22	0	0
Bolton W.	03.47	31	0	0
Blackburn Rov.	11.51	192	0	0
Northampton T.	07.56	67	0	0

ENTWISTLE, Wayne Peter
Bury, 6 August, 1958

Bury	08.76	25	6	7
Sunderland	11.77	43	2	13
Leeds U.	10.79	7	4	2
Blackpool	11.80	27	5	6
Crewe Alex.	03.82	11	0	0
Wimbledon	07.82	4	5	3
Bury	08.83	80	3	32
Carlisle U.	06.85	8	1	2
Bolton W.	10.85	5	3	0
Burnley	08.86	6	2	2
Stockport Co.	10.86	38	11	8
Bury (N/C)	08.88	0	2	0
Wigan Ath.	10.88	24	5	6
Hartlepool U.(N/C)	09.89	2	0	0

EVANS, Anthony (Tony)
Liverpool, 11 January, 1954

Blackpool	06.73	4	2	0
Cardiff C.	06.75	120	4	47
Birmingham C.	07.79	62	4	28
Crystal Palace	08.83	19	2	7
Wolverhampton W.	06.84	20	3	5
Bolton W.	02.85	4	0	0
Swindon T.	08.85	8	2	0

FARNWORTH, Simon
Chorley, 28 October, 1963

Bolton W.	09.81	113	0	0
Stockport Co.	09.86	10	0	0
Tranmere Rov.	01.87	7	0	0
Bury	03.87	105	0	0
Preston N. E.	07.90	81	0	0
Wigan Ath.	08.93	42	0	0

FARRIMOND, Sydney
Hindley, 17 July, 1940

Bolton W.	01.58	364	1	1
Tranmere Rov.	02.71	132	2	0

FELGATE, David Wynne
Blaenau Ffestiniog, 4 March, 1960

Bolton W.	08.78			
Rochdale	10.78	35	0	0
Crewe Alex.	09.79	14	0	0
Rochdale	03.80	12	0	0
Lincoln C.	09.80	198	0	0
Cardiff C.	12.84	4	0	0
Grimsby T.	02.85	36	0	0
Bolton W.	02.86	15	0	0
Bolton W.	02.87	223	0	0
Wolverhampton W.	08.93			
Chester C.	10.93	34	0	0

FISHER, Neil John
St Helens, 7 November, 1970

Bolton W.	07.89	7	6	1

FITZPATRICK, Paul James
Liverpool, 5 October, 1965

Bolton W.	03.85	13	1	0

overcoming Preston in the fifth round after three stirring encounters, then succumbing to Nottingham Forest in the last eight.

That term Lofthouse made a mockery of his birth certificate, striking 33 times in 43 League and Cup outings, a staggering return for a 33-year-old. Picture, then, poor Bill Ridding's consternation when the apparently indestructible spearhead turned his ankle in pre-season training and was ruled out for the whole of 1959/60.

In spite of this crushing blow, the Trotters contrived a sixth-place First Division finish, with only third-place Spurs boasting a better defensive record. But they suffered an inevitable shortage of goals, leaving pundits to speculate that if Lofthouse had been present the seven-point gap between Bolton and the eventual champions, Burnley, might have been bridged.

Perhaps the most positive factor to emerge from the season was the ever-increasing influence of the skilful 20-year-old Freddie Hill, a product of the club's youth policy, who made an inside-forward berth his own as Stevens took over Nat's number-nine shirt. Industrious wing-half Graham Stanley also enjoyed close to a full complement of matches as Edwards and Hennin struggled with injury, and the youngster did well.

The major disappointment was being knocked out of the FA Cup by West Bromwich Albion in the third round. In fact, it was to be the start of a dismal sequence in the competition which saw

SYD FARRIMOND
1958/59 - 1970/71

Syd Farrimond might be described, and not unkindly, as a footballer born slightly out of his time. The blond, rugged Lancastrian was a vigorous left-back whose abrasive tackling caused occasional problems with referees - he was sent off more than once - and his methods might have been more acceptable, perhaps, a decade earlier than his 1960s prime. Syd took over the number-three shirt from Tommy Banks, on whom he had modelled himself, but he didn't quite have the timing of the older man and it was inevitable that he erred from time to time. Nevertheless, the locally-born England youth international defender was a faithful and effective long-term servant of the Wanderers, for whom he signed as a 17-year-old in 1958. After contesting the left-back slot with the oft-injured Banks for two seasons, Syd was ever-present in 1961/62 and was usually in the Bolton line-up throughout the remainder of the decade. There were frequent challenges for his place, from the likes of Dave Hatton and Charlie Cooper, but he resisted them all until he was ousted first by Paul Hallows in 1969/70 and then, finally, by the promising young Don McAllister in the following season. Then Syd was given a free transfer and he settled at Tranmere Rovers, giving four terms of steady service before coaching at Halifax, Sunderland and Leeds. After that he left the game to become a newsagent at Leigh.

the Wanderers fail to progress beyond the fifth round for the next three decades and beyond.

That represented one unwelcome trend, but Bolton were about to face change of a much more radical nature.

On the playing side, 1960/61 saw Ridding's side avoid the drop into the Second Division by a mere three points, take a fourth-round FA Cup replay hammering at Blackburn and suffer an inglorious exit from the new League Cup at the hands of Second Division Rotherham

Bristol C.	08.86	40	4	7
Carlisle U.	10.88	106	3	4
Preston N. E.	12.88	2	0	0
Leicester C.	07.91	21	6	4
Birmingham C.	01.93	7	0	0
Bury	03.93	8	1	0
Northampton T. (N/C)	02.94	1	1	1

FLECK, Robert
Glasgow, 11 August, 1965

Norwich C.	12.87	130	13	40
Chelsea	08.92	35	5	3
Bolton W.	12.93	6	1	1

FLETCHER, Paul John
Bolton, 13 January, 1951

Bolton W.	11.68	33	3	5
Burnley	03.71	291	2	71
Blackpool	02.80	19	1	8

FORREST, Ernest
Sunderland, 19 February, 1919   Died 1987

Bolton W.	01.38	69	0	1
Grimsby T.	05.48	33	0	1
Millwall	06.49	37	0	4

FOSTER, Wayne Paul
Leigh, 11 September, 1963

Bolton W.	08.81	92	13	13
Preston N. E.	06.85	25	6	3

FRY, Barry F.
Bedford, 7 April, 1945

Manchester U.	04.62			
Bolton W.	05.64	3	0	1
Luton T.	07.65	6	0	0
Leyton Orient	12.66	2	1	0
Leyton Orient	06.67	5	5	0

FULTON, Stephen
Gourock, 10 August, 1970

Bolton W.	08.93	4	0	0
Peterborough U.	12.93	3	0	0

GAVIN, Mark Wilson
Baillieston, 10 December, 1963

Leeds U.	12.81	20	10	3
Hartlepool U.	03.85	7	0	0
Carlisle U.	07.85	12	1	1
Bolton W.	03.86	48	1	3
Rochdale	08.87	23	0	6
Bristol C.	10.88	62	7	6
Watford	08.90	8	5	0
Bristol C.	12.91	34	8	2
Exeter C.	02.94	12	0	0

GELDARD, Albert
Bradford, 11 April, 1914   Died 1989

Bradford P. A.	09.29	34	0	1
Everton	11.32	167	0	31
Bolton W.	06.38	29	0	1

GILLIES, Matthew Muirhead
Loganlea, 12 August, 1921

Bolton W.	10.42	145	0	1
Leicester C.	Tr01.52	103	0	0

FRANCIS LEE 1960/61 - 1967/68

Francis Lee was one of the most exciting and charismatic players who ever donned a Wanderers shirt but, from Bolton's point of view, he was born a decade too late. Had he been at Burnden Park during the 1950s, when the club was comparatively successful and cash rewards for top footballers were the same wherever they played, then Franny might have stayed to reach his magnificent peak as a Trotter. As it was he came of age in the 1960s, when the club was caught up in an inexorable slide and when the maximum wage limit had been lifted, making the grass at the big-city giants - in this case Manchester City - seem infinitely greener. Accordingly, after topping Bolton's goal charts for five successive seasons, Franny left for Maine Road in September 1967, leaving his former club to pocket a much-needed but, in hindsight, rather inadequate cheque for £65,000. The stocky, cocky utility forward was always going to hit the heights from the moment he made his League debut as a 16-year-old at home to Manchester City in November 1960. That day he scored a goal in a 3-1 victory and was even precocious enough to chide the great Nat Lofthouse for not getting on the end of several centres! That set the tone for the rest of his Burnden sojourn, during which the outspoken Lee was involved in assorted confrontations with authority and submitted several transfer requests. It said much for him, however, that whether he was on the wing, at inside-forward or leading the line, he never allowed off-the-pitch strife to interfere with the serious business of playing football. Franny was a dynamo - quick, powerful and packing a savage shot - and he formed a particularly potent spearhead with Wyn Davies. Such an ambitious individual must have been mortified by relegation to the Second Division in 1964, but still his personal standard didn't slip and the rich clubs inevitably stepped up their interest. After his switch to Maine Road, Franny became an England star and won the top domestic club honours, later also excelling with Derby County before retiring to concentrate on his parallel and mega-successful business career. In 1994 he bought a controlling interest in Manchester City; the football world awaited the outcome with baited breath.

GOULDEN, Albert Edward
Salford, 5 February, 1945

Bolton W.	02.62	1	0	0

GOWLING, Alan Edwin
Stockport, 16 March, 1949(F)

Manchester U.	04.67	64	7	18
Huddersfield T.	06.72	128	0	58
Newcastle U.	08.75	91	1	30
Bolton W.	03.78	147	2	28
Preston N. E.	09.82	37	3	5

GRAHAM, Michael A.
Lancaster, 24 February, 1959

Bolton W.	02.77	43	3	0
Swindon T.	07.81	141	0	1
Mansfield T.	07.85	132	1	1
Carlisle U.	09.88	137	1	3

GRAY, Stuart
Withernsea, 19 April, 1960

Nottingham F.	03.78	48	1	3
Bolton W.	03.83	10	0	0
Barnsley	08.83	117	3	23
Aston Villa	11.87	102	4	9
Southampton	09.91	10	2	0

GREAVES, Roy
Farnworth, 4 April, 1947

Bolton W.	01.65	487	8	66
Rochdale	11.82	19	2	0

GREEN, Scott P.
Walsall, 15 January, 1970

Derby Co.	07.88			
Bolton W.	03.90	107	39	20

GREGORY, John Charles
Scunthorpe, 11 May, 1954

Northampton T.	05.72	187	0	8
Aston Villa	06.77	59	6	10
Brighton & H.A.	07.79	72	0	7
Queens Park R.	06.81	159	2	36
Derby Co.	11.85	103	0	22
Portsmouth	07.89			
Plymouth Arg. (N/C)	01.90	3	0	0
Bolton W. (N/C)	03.90	2	5	0

GRIEVES, Kenneth John
Australia, 27 August, 1925   Died 1992

Bury	04.47	59	0	0
Bolton W.	12.51	49	0	0
Stockport Co.	07.57	39	0	0

GRIFFIN, Paul A.

Bolton W.				

GUBBINS, Ralph Grayham
Ellesmere Port, 31 January, 1932

Bolton W.	10.52	97	0	15
Hull C.	10.59	45	0	10
Tranmere Rov.	03.61	107	0	37

HALLOWS, Paul Charles Richard
Chester, 22 June, 1950

Bolton W.	10.67	45	2	0
Rochdale	05.74	197	0	2

United. As if all that was not enough, the season also marked the retirement of the most illustrious name in Wanderers' history, Nat Lofthouse, who aggravated an injury at Birmingham in December and never played another senior game.

Off the pitch, it signalled the abolition of the maximum wage and the introduction of freedom of contract, disastrous developments for town clubs such as Bolton.

Once players found themselves comparatively free in the market place, wage demands increased dramatically, causing huge financial headaches for all but the biggest fry. Before long, medium-sized clubs that in the past had been able to hang on to their prized assets - the likes of Lofthouse, Finney and Matthews - were being forced to sell, initially because they could not afford to pay the new going rate, but eventually for their very survival.

Where once Bolton had competed on equal terms with Manchester United, Everton and company, now they were involved in a one-sided struggle which, in the long term, could have only one outcome. This was a richly ironic circumstance as, towards the end of the 19th century, the Trotters had been among the prime movers at the controversial vanguard of professionalism, of which this latest development was the

WARWICK RIMMER 1960/61 - 1974/75

Warwick Rimmer was a constant, unfailingly reliable figure throughout the long Bolton decline of the 1960s, and by decade's end it seemed that every bit of his potential had been realised. Yet the doughty defensive wing-half cum centre-back confounded such judgements, reaching new levels of consistency in the early 1970s, and reaping the reward of skippering the Trotters to the Third Division title in 1972/73. An England schoolboys and youth international, Warwick was a product of the Wanderers' scouting system who made his senior debut at right-half in the club's first League Cup match, at Hull in October 1960. Stern in the tackle and blessed with a vast reservoir of stamina, he lost little time in cementing a regular place, which he was to retain, with few interruptions, until 1974. The dark-haired Merseysider was never the most ambitious of operators when the ball was at his feet, invariably preferring a short pass to an unmarked colleague or a long ball upfield. What he supplied was backbone, a much-needed commodity in Bolton's protracted rearguard actions during the first two-thirds of his Burnden career. Warwick suffered two relegations, in 1964 and 1971, and it was pleasing to all who knew this loyal servant that a Championship celebration was in store. During that successful Third Division campaign, the Rimmer experience was invaluable to young Paul Jones alongside him, and they forged a highly effective partnership. When Warwick became surplus to Ian Greaves' requirements, he joined Crewe in March 1975, going on to give four years to the Gresty Road cause. In 1981 he returned to Burnden as commercial manager, later serving Tranmere in that capacity and as youth development officer.

logical consequence.

Yet despite such an ominous watershed, it was not all doom and despondency at Burnden Park. How could it be when such an exciting talent as the precocious 16-year-old right-winger Francis Lee made his senior debut? And for good measure, callow wing-half Warwick Rimmer - destined to

play more than 500 games in a Trotters career that would last until 1974/75 - also made his first appearance. The replacement for 'Sir Nat', Irishman Billy McAdams, did well too, netting 21 times in 34 senior outings and more than justifying the £15,000 fee paid to Manchester City for his

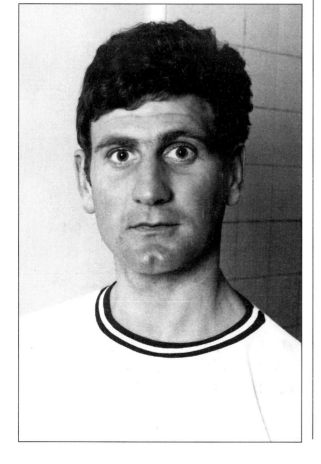

services.

Clearly, though, with new cash constraints and with the vintage 1950s side beginning to fragment, the future looked uncertain. So Burnden Park regulars had reason to be satisfied with their men's 11th place in 1961/62, a campaign which saw the £35,000 departure of Stevens to Everton where, after dropping back to midfield, he would help Alex Young *et al* lift the title in 1963. Though many supporters were sad to see him go, few could find it within their hearts to begrudge glory to such a big-hearted, underrated footballer. In any case, there was immediate compensation in the raw but immensely promising form of big Wyn Davies, a young centre-forward acquired from Wrexham for £20,000.

However, a time of inexorable travail had begun. Bolton kicked off 1962/63 dreadfully, managing only two wins in the first ten League games, though there was some consolation that one of them was a 3-0 drubbing of local giants

Manchester United. In the event, Wanderers and United were to be co-strugglers against relegation all season.

It was the winter of 'The Big Freeze', with no competitive football between early December, when Bolton squeezed an invaluable 1-0 home victory against high-riding Spurs, and mid-February, when the blanket of ice finally began to recede.

In the circumstances, it was difficult to judge the competence of a team in transition, one forced to rely on young players by economic considerations. However, there was a feeling that if the Trotters could survive this time, there was enough talent coming through to ensure a healthier future. This theory received a boost in a thrilling encounter with Sheffield United at Burnden Park in March. Not only did the home side claim both points thanks to a Freddie Hill hat-trick, they also fielded the youngest forward line in the club's history, consisting of Francis Lee (still only 18), 23-year-old Hill, Wyn Davies (20), 16-year-old debutant Brian Bromley, and Dennis Butler (18).

Neverthless, with a weather-induced May fixture pile-up to complete, Wanderers

WYN DAVIES
1961/62 - 1966/67

If Wyn Davies was hardly a household name when he arrived at Burnden Park, certainly he was when he left it. In his four and a half years as a Wanderer, the sinewy Welsh beanpole developed into the most menacing aerial attacker in the land. He scored with acceptable regularity himself, but the full scale of his contribution to the Bolton cause became apparent only when his vast number of 'assists' to fellow forward Francis Lee were considered. Bill Ridding signed 20-year-old Wyn from Wrexham for £20,000 plus Ernie Phythian in March 1962, and soon it was clear that he had acquired a gem, albeit a rather raw one. The stringy, springy striker was unable to prevent the drop to the Second Division in 1964 - in fact, he hit the target only 18 times in his first two full seasons - but he became a mainstay in the Second, notching 25 in 38 outings during 1964/65. During this period he earned the epithet 'Wyn the Leap', winning full international honours and becoming a target for any number of top clubs. Bolton fans dreaded the inevitable day of his departure, which was delayed until October 1966 when Newcastle United came in with an £80,000 offer which cash-strapped Wanderers simply had to accept. Thereafter he touched new peaks with the Magpies, tasting European triumph in the 1969 Fairs Cup competition before winding down his career with the two Manchester clubs and others. There followed a spell in South Africa before Wyn returned to Bolton, where his name will always be revered, to work in a bakery.

HAMLETT, Thomas Lawrence
Stoke, 24 January, 1917

Bolton W.	05.38	72	0	9
Port Vale	05.49	109	0	0

HANSON, Stanley
Bootle, 27 December, 1915

Bolton W.	10.35	384	0	0

HARTFORD, Richard Asa
Clydebank, 24 October, 1950

West Bromwich A.	11.67	206	8	18
Manchester C.	08.74	184	1	22
Nottingham F.	07.79	3	0	0
Everton	08.79	81	0	6
Manchester C.	10.81	75	0	7
Norwich C.	10.84	28	0	2
Bolton W.	07.85	81	0	8
Stockport Co.	06.87	42	3	0
Oldham Ath.	03.89	3	4	0
Shrewsbury T.	08.89	22	3	0

HARTLE, Leslie Roy
Bromsgrove, 4 October, 1931

Bolton W.	02.51	446	1	11

HASSALL, Harold William
Tyldesley, 4 March, 1929

Huddersfield T.	09.46	74	0	26
Bolton W.	01.52	102	0	34

HATTON, David Howcroft
Farnworth, 30 October, 1943

Bolton W.	11.60	231	0	8
Blackpool	09.69	249	1	6
Bury	08.76	96	1	2

HATTON, Robert John
Hull, 10 April, 1947

Wolverhampton W.	11.64	10	0	7
Bolton W.	03.67	23	1	2
Northampton T.	10.68	29	4	8
Carlisle U.	07.69	93	0	37
Birmingham C.	10.71	170	5	58
Blackpool	07.76	75	0	32
Luton T.	07.78	81	1	29
Sheffield U.	07.80	92	3	34
Cardiff C.	12.82	29	1	9

HEBBERD, Trevor Neil
Alresford, 19 June, 1958

Southampton	07.76	69	28	7
Bolton W.	09.81	6	0	0
Leicester C.	11.81	4	0	1
Oxford U.	03.82	260	0	37
Derby Co.	08.88	70	11	10
Portsmouth (N/C)	10.91	1	3	0
Chesterfield	11.91	67	7	1

HENDER, Reginald

Bolton W.	05.61	

HENNIN, Derek
Prescot, 28 December, 1931   Died 1987

Bolton W.	06.49	164	0	8
Chester C.	02.61	54	0	4

remained in trouble and it was only consecutive home victories over Leicester City and Liverpool that ensured safety. Winger Brian Pilkington, who had won a Championship medal at the last gasp with Burnley in 1960, found himself caught up in drama at the opposite end of the table, and proved his worth by scoring the only goal against Bill Shankly's Reds. Other results meant that Bolton finished four points clear of the trapdoor leading to the Second Division, but if anyone believed the corner had been

DAVE HATTON 1961/62 - 1969/70

The sale of Dave Hatton to Blackpool in September 1969 was a graphic illustration of the dire consequences to Bolton of the abolition of the maximum wage eight years earlier. Dave was a strong, heavy-tackling half-back in the traditional Burnden mould, the sort of trusty bulwark the struggling Trotters could ill afford to lose. But the harsh new facts of financial life meant that the offer of £40,000 for the reliable 26-year-old couldn't be refused. Locally-born Dave rose through the Burnden youth ranks and stepped on to the First Division stage for the first time at Leicester in the spring of 1962. Then came a handful of sporadic appearances as a deputy wing-half before a ten-game stint in the left-back berth as 1962/63 came to a close signalled his arrival as a genuine force. The following term saw the gritty, defensively minded Hatton settle into the middle line in the number-four shirt, though in the long term he was to become more familiar with the number six on his back. There was nothing spectacular about Dave, who contented himself with doing the simple things well. But Bolton missed him sorely when he'd gone and he excelled at Blackpool, helping his new club rise to the First Division in 1969/70, though they were demoted after just one season in the top flight. After seven years at Bloomfield Road, he became player-manager of Bury, but was sacked after a disappointing campaign in 1978/79.

turned they were in for a rude awakening come the new campaign.

Ridding's men began appallingly, with five straight League defeats. Further devastated by an injury crisis that escalated as autumn deepened into winter, they managed only three victories before Christmas, and two of them were against bottom club Ipswich Town. With five games remaining there seemed little hope of avoiding the drop, until out of the blue came three successive wins against West Ham United, Sheffield United and Chelsea, with the callow Bromley scoring

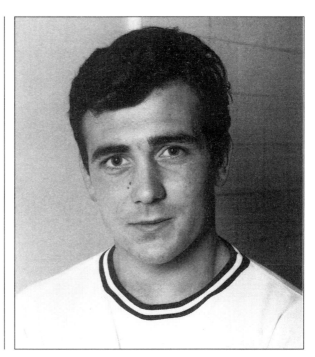

BRIAN BROMLEY 1962/63 - 1968/69

Brian Bromley was 11 days short of his 17th birthday when he stepped on to the First Division stage for the first time in March 1963. While hardly trailing clouds of glory, the neat, ball-playing inside-forward did well enough in that home clash with Sheffield United to keep his place for the next two games and there was quiet confidence at Burnden Park that the Burnley-born youngster represented genuine hope for the club's future. After all, with fellow teenagers Francis Lee and Dennis Butler alongide him, and with Wyn Davies and Freddie Hill hardly in their dotage, the Trotters were fielding an extremely youthful and spirited forward line. However, though Brian managed 18 appearances in the relegation campaign that followed - his best form coming in a late seven-game sequence as the club's lifeline slowly frayed and broke - he never matured into the influential play-maker that had been expected. Over the next five campaigns in the Second Division, the former England youth player contributed solidly enough, but no more than that, and in November 1969 he was sold to Portsmouth for £25,000. Brian's Fratton Park sojourn told a similar tale and, arguably, it was not until his move to Brighton in November 1971 that he showed signs of fulfilling that early potential. That season he helped the Seagulls rise from the Third Division, before seeing out his senior career at Reading and Darlington.

in each one. Suddenly an heroic escape was on the cards, but alas, it was not to be. A 1-0 defeat at Tottenham followed by a comprehensive 4-0 collapse against Wolves at Burnden Park consigned the Trotters to the second flight.

To a club which had spent only two seasons, 1933/34 and 1934/35, outside the First Division since 1911, it was the bitterest of blows. In the new economic climate, and in an area where competition was white hot - theChampionship pennant would leave Lancashire only once during the remainder of the decade - the possibility of permanently reduced attendances became fearfully real.

Clearly it was of paramount importance for Bolton to bounce back quickly, and what a spirited effort they made to rejoin the elite at the first attempt. With half the 1958 rearguard still intact - Hopkinson, Hartle and Edwards - and jointly spearheaded by 23-goal Lee and Davies, who contributed 21, they were among the leaders throughout the season. Sadly they fell away

alarmingly at the death, scoring only twice in their last five games, to finish third behind Newcastle United and Northampton Town.

The FA Cup brought an

exhilarating distraction, however. First little Workington Town were swept aside, then a 2-1 victory over Preston at Deepdale brought sweet revenge for defeat at the

ROY GREAVES
1965/66 - 1979/80

Roy Greaves was a hero in Bolton - eventually. At his peak he was a splendidly accomplished midfielder, coveted by the likes of Liverpool and Arsenal, and he skippered the Wanderers to the Second Division title in 1977/78. But before the bouquets began raining deservedly on his head, he had to endure his share of brickbats. Local boy Roy began his Trotters career at centre-forward, netting twice on his home League debut against Southampton in the autumn of 1965. However, over the next few terms, at a time when the side was beginning to deteriorate, he failed to win over his home fans (despite leading the club's goal charts for two seasons) and was subjected to mindless criticism. The turning point came when new manager Jimmy Armfield withdrew him to midfield after relegation to the Third Division in 1971. In the deeper role, a slight lack of pace was less noticeable and his neat distribution, strength and industry were displayed to full advantage. Burly Roy was a key component of the combination that topped the Third Division in 1972/73 and, as his engine-room partnership with Peter Reid blossomed in mid-decade, he continued to grow in influence. Even though he had moved back, the powerful Greaves shot remained in evidence, never more so than when his 20-yarder decided the home encounter with Spurs in November 1977 and confirmed the Wanderers as serious promotion contenders. Stepping out in the top flight for the first time in 1978/79, Roy held his own, but a combination of injuries and advancing years saw his long and honourable Burnden tenure draw to a close in 1980. There followed a stint with Seattle before he played and coached at Rochdale, then ran a pub back in his beloved Bolton.

hands of their local rivals in the corresponding round a year earlier. That set up a titanic clash with League champions Liverpool and the 57,000-plus who bulged Burnden's seams savoured a truly gripping contest.

When the Merseysiders' colossal centre-half Ron Yeats

Houghton-le-Spring, 26 November, 1957

Manchester C.	12.74	68	11	6
Bolton W.	09.81	70	0	22
Oldham Ath.	03.83	185	5	25
Stoke C.	12.87	59	3	11
Shrewsbury T.	08.91	39	1	7

HENSHAW, Gary
Leeds, 18 February, 1965

Grimsby T.	02.83	46	4	9
Bolton W.	06.87	49	21	4
Rochdale	03.90	8	1	1

HERNON, James
Cleland, 6 December, 1924

Leicester C.	04.42	31	0	7
Bolton W.	09.48	43	0	2
Grimsby T.	08.51	91	0	23
Watford	07.54	43	0	10

HIGGINS, George
Dundee, 16 June, 1925

Blackburn Rov.	10.46	53	0	0
Bolton W.	07.51	69	0	0
Grimsby T.	05.54	47	0	0

HIGGINS, John Oldfield
Bakewell, 15 November, 1932

Bolton W.	10.50	183	0	0

HILL, Frederick
Sheffield, 17 January, 1940

Bolton W.	03.57	373	2	74
Halifax T.	07.69	25	0	3
Manchester C.	05.70	28	7	3
Peterborough U.	08.73	73	2	7

HOGGAN, David M.
Falkirk, 10 August, 1961

Bolton W.	08.79	83	10	11

HOLDEN, Albert Douglas
Manchester, 28 September, 1930

Bolton W.	01.50	419	0	40
Preston N.E.	11.62	89	0	13

HOPKINSON, Edward
Royton, 29 October, 1935

Oldham Ath. (Am)	06.51	3	0	0
Bolton W.	11.52	519	0	0

HOULT, Russell
Leicester, 22 November, 1972

Leicester C.	03.91	10	0	0
Lincoln C.	08.91	2	0	0
Bolton W.	11.93	3	1	0

HOWE, Donald
Wakefield, 26 November, 1917

Bolton W.	11.34	266	0	35

HUBBICK, Henry (Harry)
Jarrow, 12 November, 1914   Died 1992

Burnley	03.35	58	0	1
Bolton W.	02.37	128	0	0
Port Vale	10.47	50	0	1
Rochdale	01.49	90	0	0

strained a muscle early in the first half, it seemed Bolton might claim a crucial advantage through the aerial menace of 'Wyn The Leap'. But the Scottish stopper turned in one of his grittiest performances to subdue Davies, and Ian Callaghan secured a quarter-final place for the eventual Cup-winners with a goal only five minutes from time.

On paper the Wanderers appeared to be among the favourites for promotion in 1965/66, but in reality, perhaps, more new blood was needed than Ridding had the financial resources to provide. Though Hopkinson and the excellent Hill - who was unsettled at Burnden but for whom repeated transfer talk didn't materialise into a move - continued to play well, Lee and Davies managed only 13 League goals apiece, Edwards had retired and Hartle was no longer quite the same formidable force.

On the credit side, one or two local lads, notably forward Roy Greaves, were beginning to show distinct signs of maturing into good-quality pros, at the very least. However, they were not far enough advanced to avert an anti-climactic campaign which saw the Trotters end up in mid-table, never threatening seriously to join the promotion battle. In the Cup, they met Preston in the fourth round for the third successive year, this particular mini-series being settled in the Deepdale men's favour by two victories to one.

As the halcyon First

Division days grew ever more distant, the pressure on Ridding to transform the club's fortunes grew, but eroding gates rendered the task increasingly daunting. The veteran of 15 years at the Burnden helm battled on gamely, though, recruiting Blackburn striker John Byrom to relieve some of the scoring pressure from the Davies-Lee tandem. However, before long Newcastle made an £80,000 offer for the Welsh international which

---

GORDON TAYLOR
1962/63 - 1970/71

The best years of Gordon Taylor's not inconsiderable playing career, which tends to be overshadowed by his subsequent achievements as secretary of the Professional Footballers Association, were spent at Bolton. Though the diminutive Lancastrian gave notable subsequent service to Birmingham, and contributed brief but sterling stints to Blackburn and Bury, he never quite recaptured the spirited form of his Burnden Park days. Gordon, who joined the Trotters straight from school, was reminiscent in style to his bustling contemporary, Francis Lee, who lined up on the opposite right flank in the early 1960s. Of course, while both were short and squarely built, both could cross beautifully and both relished cutting in from the touchline for a shot, Gordon was never in Franny's exalted class. Nevertheless, he showed much promise in 1963/64, the first term in which he was granted a run of senior appearances, only for the season to be blighted by relegation from the top flight. Over the next six and a half campaigns, Gordon was a leading light, especially in 1964/65 when Bolton came close to bouncing back to the First Division at the first attempt. Sadly, come December 1970, with demotion to the Third beckoning and the club in dire financial straits, he was sold to Birmingham for the ludicrously low fee of £18,000. He retired as a player in 1979, since when he has won wide respect for his PFA work. Gordon Taylor knows the game at all levels and can be expected to contribute hugely to its administration in the years ahead.

HUGHES, Paul
Denton, 19 December, 1968

Bolton W.	07.87	12	1	0

HUGHES, William
Ballymena (NI), 9 May, 1929

Bolton W.	08.48	47	0	2
Bournemouth	06.53	16	0	1

HULME, John
Mobberley, 6 February, 1945

Bolton W.	02.62	186	2	7
Notts Co.	03.72	8	0	0
Reading	07.72	86	1	0
Bury	07.74	86	0	5

HUNT, George Samuel
Barnsley, 22 February, 1910

Chesterfield	09.29	14	0	9
Tottenham H.	06.30	185	0	125
Arsenal	10.37	18	0	3
Bolton W.	02.38	45	0	24
Sheffield Wed.	11.46	32	0	8

HUNT, Roger
Golborne, 20 July, 1938

Liverpool	05.59	401	3	245
Bolton W.	12.69	72	4	24

HURLEY, Charles J.
Cork, 4 October, 1936

Millwall	10.53	105	0	2
Sunderland	09.57	357	1	23
Bolton W.	06.69	41	1	3

HURST, (Jack)
Bolton, 27 October, 1914

Bolton W.	05.33	60	0	2
Oldham Ath.	02.47	98	0	2

JACKSON, James
Glasgow, 1 January, 1921

Bolton W.	06.39	11	0	1
Carlisle U.	07.50	100	0	22

JEFFREY, Michael Richard
Liverpool, 11 August, 1971

Bolton W.	02.89	9	6	0
Doncaster Rov.	03.92	48	1	19
Newcastle U.	10.93	2	0	0

JEMSON, Nigel Bradley
Preston, 10 August, 1969

Preston N.E.	07.87	28	4	8
Nottingham F.	03.88	45	2	13
Bolton W.	12.88	4	1	0
Preston N.E.	03.89	6	3	2
Sheffield Wed.	09.91	26	25	9
Grimsby T.	09.93	6	0	2

JONES, Gary Edwin
Wythenshawe, 11 December, 1950

Bolton W.	01.68	195	8	41
Sheffield U.	02.75	3	0	1
Blackpool	11.78	18	9	5
Hereford U.	08.80	21	4	4

Bolton could not afford to refuse, and undoubtedly Davies' departure was a major factor in another mediocre campaign.

Worse was to follow in 1967/68 when Wanderers parted with Francis Lee - their most effective and charismatic performer since Lofthouse and leading scorer for five successive seasons - to Manchester City.

In retrospect, selling the fiery flankman-cum-striker for £65,000 and replacing him with an admirable enough but less accomplished player, Terry Wharton of Wolves, for £70,000 makes little sense. No doubt the time was ripe for Lee to leave - he was not always the easiest individual to handle and his marvellous talent deserved the wider stage it found for his new club and his country - but the two deals did not add up to good value for a club struggling to rise from the middle reaches of the Second Division.

The manager, who had also spent £50,000 on wing-half Gareth Williams from Cardiff City, continued to suffer dire frustration as the Trotters completed a lacklustre season in 12th place. The fact that

JOHN BYROM 1966/67 - 1975/76

John Byrom was a folk hero, no less, at Bolton in the late 1960s and early 1970s. An instinctive goal-scorer with an easy-going character who struck up a rare rapport with the Burnden Park crowd, he might have achieved even more in the game with a ruthless approach. But then he wouldn't have been 'JB'. Bill Ridding signed John from Blackburn Rovers, his hometown club, for £25,000 in that hallowed summer of 1966, when most fans' attention was on England's World Cup exploits. Initially he linked promisingly with Davies and Lee, but Wyn and then Franny departed and no replacements of similar calibre were brought in. This left John with a mammoth responsibility, which he shouldered manfully but without achieving the hoped-for prolific returns. However, come 1969/70, with Wanderers well entrenched in the wrong half of the table, he found a new gear and notched 25 senior goals at a time when they were sorely needed. Sadly, relegation followed and John was deployed frequently in a deep-lying role during 1971/72 so the goals did not flow freely. But back up front in 1972/73, he was rampant once more, netting 20 times to help lift the Third Division title, then scoring 18 times in only 32 League starts during the first term back in the Second. Never was the essence of 'JB' demonstrated more vividly than in an FA Cup battle with Stoke at Burnden in January 1973. Bolton had forged into a 3-0 lead, courtesy of a Byrom hat-trick, when John Ritchie netted twice for the Potters. Then, late in the game, Ritchie nodded what looked to be a certain equaliser, but up popped 'JB' to clear off the line, then salute the fans in rousing gladiatorial fashion. Another example of his prowess and his spirit came when he ploughed through the mud from halfway to grab a late equaliser at Southampton during that same Cup run. Often John, who grappled with a weight problem at times, struggled on with injuries and the supporters loved him for it. When he was given a free transfer in 1976 - he returned to Ewood Park for a brief Indian summer - the Burnden Park scene was the poorer for his absence.

Greaves was top scorer with only ten League goals spoke volumes.

Change was imperative if Bolton were not to slide gently into oblivion, and it came in August 1968 when Bill Ridding announced that after nearly 18 years in the Burnden Park hot seat (and 22 at the club including his post-war stint as trainer) he was resigning to ply his trade as a physiotherapist. Though his final period in charge had been disappointing, due mainly to the changing facts of football life, Bill had presided over a golden era in Bolton Wanderers history. It would be nothing less than monstrous if his subsequent travails in reduced circumstances were allowed to obscure those splendid earlier achievements.

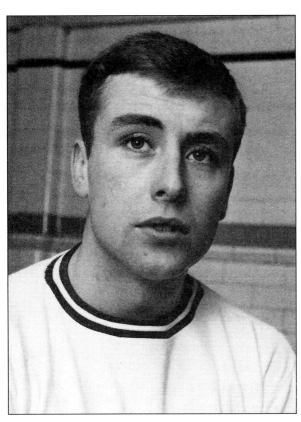

JONES, Paul Bernard
Ellesmere Port, 13 May, 1953

Bolton W.	06.70	441	4	38
Huddersfield T.	07.83	73	0	8
Oldham Ath.	12.85	32	0	1
Blackpool	03.87	31	6	0
Rochdale	03.89	14	0	2
Stockport Co.	06.89	25	0	0

JOYCE, Warren Garton
Oldham, 20 January, 1965

Bolton W.	06.82	180	4	17
Preston N.E.	10.87	170	7	34
Plymouth Arg.	05.92	28	2	3
Burnley	07.93	19	3	4

KEELEY, Glenn Mathew
Barking, 1 September, 1954

Ipswich T.	08.72	4	0	0
Newcastle U.	07.74	43	1	2
Blackburn Rov.	08.76	365	5	23
Everton	10.82	1	0	0
Oldham Ath.	08.87	10	1	0
Colchester U.	02.88	4	0	0
Bolton W.	09.88	20	0	0

KELLY, Anthony Gerald
Prescot, 1 January, 1964

Liverpool	09.82			
Wigan Ath.	01.84	98	3	15
Stoke C.	04.86	33	3	4
West Bromwich A.	07.87	26	0	1
Chester C.	09.88	5	0	0
Colchester U.	10.88	13	0	2
Shrewsbury T.	01.89	100	1	15
Bolton W.	08.91	99	3	5

KENNEDY, Andrew John
Stirling, 8 October, 1964

Birmingham C.	03.85	51	25	19
Sheffield U.	03.87	8	1	1
Blackburn Rov.	06.88	49	10	23
Watford	08.90	17	8	4
Bolton W.	10.91	1	0	0
Brighton & H.A.	09.92	34	8	10

KENNEDY, Gordon McKay
Dundee, 15 April, 1924

Blackpool	10.43	8	0	0
Bolton W.	09.50	17	0	0
Stockport Co.	08.53	20	0	1

KIDD, Brian
Manchester, 29 May, 1949

Manchester U.	06.66	195	8	52
Arsenal	08.74	77	0	30
Manchester C.	07.76	97	1	44
Everton	03.79	40	0	12
Bolton W.	05.80	40	3	14

KINSELL, Thomas Henry
Cannock, 3 May, 1921

West Bromwich A.	06.38	83	0	0
Bolton W.	06.49	17	0	0
Reading	05.50	12	0	0
West Ham U.	01.51	101	0	2

LANGLEY, Geoffrey Ralph
Gateshead, 31 March, 1962

Bolton W.	03.80	3	3	0

In this hour of need, the Trotters turned to a man who had a better chance than most of capturing the public imagination and thereby motivating a revival. The problem was that Nat Lofthouse, on his own subsequent admission, was never cut out to be a manager. Though he had enjoyed his work as chief coach during the final year of Ridding's reign, fundamentally he was too nice to make the often-painful decisions that are the unenviable lot of a soccer boss.

At first Lofthouse took the job on a temporary basis, making the arrangement permanent in December, but many who knew him well predicted that it would not work. At first, he seemed to be proving the doubters wrong, guiding his side to a bright start with only one defeat in the opening six League matches. But by early winter the grim reality that the team was not good enough was harrowingly apparent, and they nosedived to finish a poor 17th in the table.

Lofthouse reacted

JOHN RITSON
1967/68 - 1977/78

John Ritson was a thoroughly modern full-back, one of Bolton's first. He relished galloping down the right flank to deliver a cross or, better still, to unleash one of his characteristically thunderous blasts at goal. Though he netted only 13 times in 378 senior outings, the compact Merseysider was always a threat, his relish for going forward perhaps a legacy of earlier days in midfield. In fact, John's first senior appearance, as an 18-year-old in the autumn of 1967, was made in the number-seven shirt worn until two weeks earlier by Francis Lee. But it was at number-two that he would carve his long-term niche, becoming a regular in 1968/69 and generally holding sway until injuries began to undermine him in 1976/77. By then John had shared in the disappointment of relegation to the Third in 1971, been a stalwart when the Trotters bounced back two years later, and was still on hand to claim a Second Division Championship medal for his 19 outings in 1977/78. However, he was not to be given a chance in the top flight, the right-back role being entrusted to Peter Nicholson, and in September 1978 he was sold to Bury for £25,000. Two terms at Gigg Lane were followed by a Burnden return, but he never rose above the reserve ranks in this second spell and soon left the professional game. John Ritson was never a star name but he is recalled with affection by Wanderers fans as an efficient defender with an endearing penchant for adventure.

positively by recruiting experienced players to blend with a crop of promising youngsters. In came the England World Cup hero, Roger Hunt of Liverpool, Republic of Ireland international Charlie Hurley (reckoned by many shrewd observers to have been the finest centre-half in Britain during his Sunderland prime) and striker John Manning from Norwich City, but injuries reduced their effectiveness, the balance was never right and 1969/70 saw an improvement of only

one place.

Now the writing was on the wall and the message was unpalatable in the extreme: unless the current trend was reversed, Bolton would soon be sampling Third Division soccer for the first time, an unthinkable prospect for those who had followed them in their 1950s pomp.

Yet Lofthouse's men, now coached by former Burnley and Northern Ireland schemer Jimmy McIlroy, started 1970/71 with a flourish, winning their first two games and

LANGTON, Robert
Burscough, 8 September, 1918

Blackburn Rov.	09.38	107	0	24
Preston N.E.	08.48	55	0	14
Bolton W.	11.49	118	0	16
Blackburn Rov.	09.53	105	0	33

LEE, David Mark
Blackburn, 5 November, 1967

Bury	08.86	203	5	35
Southampton	08.91	11	9	0
Bolton W.	11.92	67	6	10

LEE, Francis Henry
Westhoughton, 29 April, 1944

Bolton W.	05.61	189	0	92
Manchester C.	10.67	248	1	112
Derby Co.	08.74	62	0	24

LEE, Samuel
Liverpool, 7 February, 1959

Liverpool	04.76	190	7	13
Queens Park R.	08.86	29	1	0
Southampton	01.90	0	2	0
Bolton W.	10.90	4	0	0

LEE, F. Stuart
Manchester, 11 February, 1953

Bolton W.	02.71	77	8	20
Wrexham	11.75	46	8	12
Stockport Co.	08.78	49	0	21
Manchester C.	09.79	6	1	2

LEES, Alfred
Worsley, 28 July, 1923

Bolton W.	05.47	2	0	0
New Brighton	08.49	72	0	0
Crewe Alex.	09.51	185	0	5

LENNARD, David
Manchester, 31 December, 1944

Bolton W.	12.61	114	5	3
Halifax T.	07.69	97	0	16
Blackpool	10.71	42	3	9
Cambridge U.	08.73	39	1	6
Chester C.	09.74	73	2	11
Stockport Co.	07.76	39	0	4
Bournemouth	09.77	56	3	4

LODGE, Paul
Liverpool, 13 February, 1961

Everton	02.79	20	4	0
Wigan Ath.	08.82	5	0	1
Rotherham U.	01.83	4	0	0
Preston N.E.	02.83	36	2	0
Bolton W.	07.84	4	0	0
Port Vale	11.84	3	0	0
Stockport Co.	03.85	10	3	2

LOFTHOUSE, Nathaniel (Nat)
Bolton, 27 August, 1925

Bolton W.	08.42	452	0	255

LYDIATE, Jason L.
Manchester, 29 October, 1971

Manchester U.	07.90			
Bolton W.	03.92	12	0	0

scoring six times in the process. Sadly it was to prove a false dawn with only three more victories garnered before November, when McIlroy assumed control of the team and Lofthouse moved upstairs as general manager.

The good-natured Ulsterman, a former Oldham Athletic boss and Stoke City coach, was to occupy the seat of power for just 18 days before resigning when it became apparent that the cash-strapped board wanted to sell some of his best players. Harsh economic necessities were involved but McIlroy felt that building for the future in such straitened circumstances was simply not on.

Back downstairs to hold the fort came the faithful Lofthouse and he was rewarded a day later with a morale-boosting home victory over Birmingham City, thanks to a hat-trick from the old warhorse Hunt. Nat had made it clear, though, that his guidance of team affairs must be a temporary arrangement and the need for new leadership

was emphasised by another sequence of dismal results which embedded the Trotters deep in the relegation mire. And far from offering relief from the slog for League points, the FA Cup brought yet

more distress in the form of a 2-0 defeat at Fourth Division York City.

Come mid-January the directors had decided that the Blackpool coach and ex-Stockport County manager Jimmy Meadows was their man.

GARRY JONES
1968/69 - 1978/79

Garry Jones lingers in the memory as the prototype 1970s footballer, with his longish hair, light beard and generally 'modern' image, an impression made all the more striking by his contrast with fellow marksman John Byrom, emphatically one of the old school. Garry was a Mancunian who turned his back on both United and City to throw in his lot with the Wanderers, becoming a professional in January 1968 and making his senior debut some 14 months later. He did not establish himself until the early months of 1971, after which he was an automatic choice for the next two seasons before settling for an in-and-out status for most of the decade. Slim and nippy, useful in the air and an efficient penalty-taker, Garry was never the heaviest of scorers and was ideally suited to the role of secondary striker. In fairness, though, a lot of his goals tended to be important ones, especially during the 1972/73 Third Division title-winning campaign, when he hit the target 14 times. Then there was his hat-trick which dumped Manchester City out of the League Cup in October 1971, a supremely satisfying night's work against his hometown club. He proved an able foil for both Byrom and then Neil Whatmore, though it was the latter's rise which cost Garry his regular place. The final straw that signalled the end of his Burnden tenure was the signing of Frank Worthington, soon after which, in November 1978 and still only 27, he switched to Blackpool. However, there was little joy for Garry at Bloomfield Road and he moved on to Hereford before entering the non-League ranks.

The former England international, a native of Bolton, found grounds for optimism as his first match in charge produced an uplifting 2-1 home triumph over high-flying Sheffield United. True the team, consisting mainly of youngsters, had been selected by Lofthouse, but the points offered a welcome platform on which to build.

Unfortunately, the new edifice never got off the ground. That win, on January 16, proved to be the last of the season and 11 weeks later Meadows followed McIlroy out of the Burnden Park door. He had presided over a turbulent interlude which had seen important players, the talented young forward Paul Fletcher and experienced winger Terry Wharton, leave the club and several others demand transfers.

Meanwhile Wanderers were at the foot of the table and when Lofthouse resumed as caretaker in early April there was no realistic hope of escaping the drop. In the end, Bolton collected the Second Division's wooden spoon, accumulating a mere 24 points (seven short of safety) and netting only 35 goals while conceding 74. There was no doubt about it, they deserved their fate, but that made it no easier to accept for the hardcore of fans (on one occasion, at home to Sunderland, fewer than 6,000 of them) who remained loyal to the last.

When such a slide is under way, there is always the disturbing

ROGER HUNT
1969/70 - 1971/72

When Bolton signed England World Cup hero Roger Hunt from Liverpool in December 1969, they got more for their £32,000 than a star name. They had acquired a man with a special place in his heart for the Wanderers, the club he had supported as a boy growing up in nearby Golborne. Sadly, Roger found the team at a low ebb and although he worked hard alongside fellow striker John Byrom, his first season at Burnden ended with Bolton entrenched firmly in the wrong half of the Second Division. Matters grew worse the following term and the former idol of the Anfield Kop found himself in and out of the side as it struggled unavailingly to avoid relegation. Roger showed his spirit, however, and provided a pinprick of light in the gloom when he responded to one period on the sidelines by returning with a second-half hat-trick at home to Birmingham City. That was an isolated success, though, and he found himself performing at Third Division venues in 1971/72. But, far from despairing, Roger revealed his mettle both as a footballer and a man. That season he worked prodigiously, shrugging off the burden of being a prime target for some of his more physical opponents, and he finished as the club's joint top-scorer in the League with 11 goals. After that, with his 34th birthday looming and a future in the family haulage business on his mind, Roger retired. He left with the satisfaction that he had helped to steady the Wanderers (they were only just off the promotion pace) at a time when, all too easily, the slump might have continued. Many fans rued the fact that he didn't stay for one more campaign. As it was Roger Hunt left with honour, secure in the knowledge that he had given good value for money to the very last.

possibility that it will continue indefinitely. Happily, though, a nadir had been reached and May brought the appointment that was to point Wanderers in the right direction once more. Former England captain Jimmy Armfield arrived from Blackpool, his sole club and where lately he had been player-coach, and immediately there was a new sense of optimism and stability about Burnden Park.

He had inherited a side in disarray and set about remedying the situation by building from the back, recruiting defenders Henry Mowbray and Peter Nicholson from Bloomfield Road, and goalkeeper Charlie Wright from Charlton Athletic. Integrating them skilfully with his existing, mostly youthful staff, Armfield consolidated and Bolton ended his first management season in a useful seventh place. Indeed, but for an early-season run of only two wins in 16 outings, they would have been among the promotion challengers. Spice was added through creditable runs in both major Cup

competitions, the Trotters going out to Chelsea in both, and sound foundations had been laid for a happier future.

Those longed-for better days materialised in 1972/73 when Armfield's good sense and enterprise paid rich dividends. With chief

72

marksman Byrom equalling his best League tally of 20 goals, Bolton took the Third Division title by a comfortable four-point

margin, netting 73 times to 38 against. In addition they reached the fifth round of the FA Cup, playing nine times including replays, before

DON McALLISTER
1969/70 - 1974/75

Bolton's bone-shaking tacklers of the 1950s might have indulged in a moment or two of misty-eyed nostalgia when they watched young Don McAllister in action. Here was a lad in the true tradition of the Burnden Park academy for tough nuts, a powerful, uncompromising defender who would never be found wanting for aggression and guts. The blond left-footer, who captained the Trotters youth team to Lancashire Cup triumph in 1970, was equally at home in central defence or at left-back and gave yeoman service to the Wanderers' cause throughout the first half of the decade. Don made his senior debut in spring 1970, then claimed Syd Farrimond's number-three shirt on a regular basis come the following November and was part of the team that descended to the Third Division. However, he was still in his teens with plenty to learn, and lost the job temporarily to Henry Mowbray for the first half of 1971/72. Thereafter, he was in the side for keeps, contributing lustily to the Third Division title effort in 1972/73. After the arrival of Tony Dunne during 1973/74, Don shifted to a central role alongside Paul Jones and also proved adept as a man-to-man marker - few play-makers prospered when he gave them his undivided attention. Such was the McAllister progress that he took the eye of richer clubs, and in February 1975 he joined Spurs for £80,000, leaving Jones, Sam Allardyce and Mike Walsh to contest berths in Bolton's central rearguard. The Londoners were happy with their acquisition, who made more than 200 appearances during a traumatic period for the club. Ironically, when the Trotters lost at White Hart Lane in a promotion battle in April 1978, Don scored the only goal. He completed his career with Charlton, Tampa Bay and Rochdale.

McADAMS, William John
Belfast, 20 January, 1934

Manchester C.	12.53	127	0	62
Bolton W.	09.60	44	0	26
Leeds U.	12.61	11	0	3
Brentford	07.62	75	0	36
Queens Park R.	09.64	33	0	13
Barrow	07.66	53	0	9

McALLISTER, Donald
Radcliffe, 26 May, 1953

Bolton W.	06.70	155	1	2
Tottenham H.	02.75	168	4	9
Charlton Ath.	08.81	55	0	6
Rochdale (N/C)	11.84	3	0	0

McATEER, Jason Wynne
Birkenhead, 18 June, 1971

Bolton W.	01.92	64	3	3

McBURNEY, Michael Leslie
Wrexham, 12 September, 1953

Wrexham	07.71	20	4	4
Bolton W.	05.73	1	0	0
Hartlepool U.	11.74	5	1	1
Tranmere Rov.	03.75	4	1	0

McDONAGH, James Martin (Seamus)
Rotherham, 6 October, 1952

Rotherham U.	10.70	121	0	0
Bolton W.	08.76	161	0	0
Everton	07.80	40	0	0
Bolton W.	08.81	81	0	1
Notts Co.	07.83	35	0	0
Birmingham C.	09.84	1	0	0
Gillingham	03.85	10	0	0
Sunderland	08.85	7	0	0
Scarborough	11.87	9	0	0
Huddersfield T.	01.88	6	0	0
Charlton Ath.	03.88			

McELHINNEY, Gerard
Derry (NI), 19 September, 1956

Bolton W.	09.80	107	2	2
Rochdale	11.82	20	0	1
Plymouth Arg.	01.85	90	1	2
Peterborough U.	08.88	87	0	1

McGARRY, Ronald James
Whitehaven, 5 December, 1937

Workington	10.58	92	0	25
Bolton W.	02.62	27	0	7
Newcastle U.	12.62	118	3	41
Barrow	03.67	30	0	4
Barrow	09.70	14	3	4

McGINLEY, John
Inverness, 8 April, 1964

Shrewsbury T.	02.89	58	2	27
Bury	07.90	16	9	9
Millwall	03.91	27	7	10
Bolton W.	09.92	70	3	41

McGOVERN, John Prescott
Montrose, 28 October, 1949

Hartlepool U.	05.67	69	3	5
Derby Co.	09.68	186	4	16
Leeds U.	08.74	4	0	0
Nottingham F.	02.75	249	4	6
Bolton W.	06.82	16	0	0

falling victim to Luton Town. The men who brought the pride back to Burnden were 'keeper Charlie Wright, defenders John Ritson, Paul Jones, Warwick Rimmer (skipper) and Don McAllister, utility man Peter Nicholson, midfielders Roy Greaves and Alan Waldron, and forwards John Byrom, Garry Jones, Stuart Lee and Ron Phillips.

By now, Armfield was one of the most sought-after young bosses in the business and big clubs began beating a path to his door. But he was to

PAUL JONES 1970/71 - 1982/83

No finer footballing centre-half has graced Bolton Wanderers since the war than Paul Jones. He patrolled the rearguard with Alan Hansen-like aplomb, never the quickest of movers but skilful on the ball, perceptive in his passing and effective in the air. He was dangerous going forward, too, netting no fewer than 11 League goals in 1976/77, including four penalties. Not surprisingly, there was a time during Don Revie's mid-1970s reign as England boss that the tall pivot was called into the national squad, and many Trotters fans believe to this day that his failure to win a full cap was outrageous. Paul, who joined Bolton on leaving school, was given a handful of senior outings in 1970/71, then he consolidated his progress the following term. Such was his all-round ability that some of his early games were played in midfield, but before long he settled at the back. In 1972/73 Paul was an ever-present as Bolton topped the Third, then he proceeded to miss no more than a handful of matches for all but one of the next ten seasons. Ironically that was in 1977/78, when injury sidelined him for several months as Ian Greaves' side lifted the Second Division title. Happily, though, he did qualify for a medal. In the top flight, Paul showed his versatility with a spell at right-back, but lacked the pace to fill the role regularly. He remained a Trotter as the club took a nosedive, finally leaving for Huddersfield after demotion to the Third in 1983. Down the years, various top clubs expressed interest in him and he had several transfer requests turned down. Bolton could be thankful that they enjoyed the services of such a classy performer for so long.

remain at Burnden for one more term, long enough for the Wanderers to find their feet in the Second Division and provide a springboard for greater things ahead. Shrewdly, the pipe-smoking Lancastrian realised that his team, worthy though they were, needed an injection of class to do well at the higher level in which they now found themselves, and to that end he signed full-back Tony Dunne from Manchester United and winger Peter Thompson from Liverpool. Though

PETER NICHOLSON 1971/72 - 1981/82

Peter Nicholson never played in goal for Bolton, but had he done so the chances are he would have acquitted himself admirably. The basis for such confidence is that the likeable, loyal Cumbrian was a natural athlete and ball-player who wore every other shirt for the Wanderers during an acomplished 11-year stay at Burnden Park and, to varying degrees, seemed at home in all of them. Peter signed for Bolton in June 1971 in a low-key £4,000 deal, the first completed by Jimmy Armfield in his new capacity as Bolton boss. The two men had played together at Bloomfield Road and Jimmy knew he was getting marvellous value for money. So it proved as Peter made more than 350 appearances during the rest of the decade and beyond, perhaps being most fitted to the right-back role, though he was also extremely capable as a one-on-one marker in midfield. Presented with any specific task, he would give it his all, and let no one doubt that he brought considerable footballing skill to his work. Peter could control the ball surely and pass it smoothly, and was also a shrewd interceptor. He shared in the Third Division title triumph of 1973, the Second Division Championship five years later, then held his own in the top flight and was still on hand to strive valiantly but unsuccessfully against demotion in 1980. Peter was brave, too, sometimes struggling on with injuries such as a broken wrist in 1981/82, his final term as a Trotter. There followed brief stints with Rochdale and Carlisle before Peter retired, but his heart remained at Bolton, where he was coaching the schoolboys and helping with commercial activities in 1994.

both men were on the wrong side of 30, they fully justified Armfield's judgement, and helped the club to a satisfactory 11th place in 1973/74.

In September 1974 the moment Bolton supporters had been dreading finally arrived when Armfield bade farewell, taking over the reins of Leeds United from Brian Clough. Jimmy was replaced by his assistant, Ian Greaves, the peak of whose management career to date had been taking Huddersfield into the First Division, though he was also in charge as they plummeted subsequently into the Third.

Greaves made a chequered start as Bolton boss, frequently shuffling his pack in that first autumn but gradually settling on a formation which saw the team to tenth position in the table come season's end. By now the likes of midfielder Peter Reid, central defender Sam Allardyce and striker Neil Whatmore were becoming established and a team was taking shape that was destined to restore, for a time, a

measure of former glories.

Season 1975/76 started inauspiciously, with defeats at Bristol City and Oxford United. But there were no further

reverses until late November and, in the spring, the Trotters were battling boldly for promotion. Agonisingly, they finished a point behind

West Bromwich Albion, who went up in third place, and were left to reflect on the consequences of a shock home defeat by lowly York City in mid-April.

Bolton confirmed their growing stature in the FA Cup, too, First Division Newcastle eliminating them in the fifth round but only at the third attempt.

NEIL WHATMORE
1972/73 - 1980/81 and 1982/83-1983/84

Neil Whatmore's first goal for Bolton was a crucial strike, one of a brace on his debut at Swansea as the Trotters were straining towards the Third Division title in April 1973. His last was at Burnley 11 years later, securing a draw in an inconsequential middle-of-the-table clash in that same third flight. In between, this honest, efficient journeyman striker had hit the target more than 100 times, holding his own in each of the top three divisions. Sandy-haired Neil had made that dramatic appearance at The Vetch when still a teenage amateur, thus completing his progress through Bolton's youth ranks. During the mid-1970s Ian Greaves slotted him into the side which pushed regularly for elevation to the First and he prospered, notably in 1976/77 when he supplied 31 goals in senior competitions. Adept at controlling the ball and turning neatly, Neil was useful in the air and ever willing to battle for scraps. Usually he enjoyed a friendly rapport with the fans, though he became a victim of their ire in times of frustration. Having netted 19 times during the Second Division title term of 1978, Neil found himself pushed back to midfield to accommodate Gowling and Worthington the following season, but was called forward again in 1979/80. To many, that was when he proved his true worth, scoring 18 goals for a poor side against the best defences around. Still, Wanderers went down and in 1981 Whatmore joined Birmingham for £340,000, a record sale for the club. However, he was unsettled at St Andrews, returning to Bolton briefly on loan in December 1982, as he did again in March 1984 when an Oxford player. There followed spells with Burnley and Mansfield before he put in his fourth stint at Burnden, this time in 1987/88 after an anonymous fan came up with his wages, but he never made the first team.

McILWAINE, Matthew
Glasgow, 20 September, 1920

Bolton W.	08.51	2	0	0

McMAHON, Kevin
Tantobie, 1 March, 1946

Newcastle U.	08.67			
York C.	05.69	85	8	31
Bolton W.	03.72	4	2	1
Barnsley	07.73	104	3	28

McNAB, Neil
Greenock, 4 June, 1957

Tottenham H.	02.74	63	9	3
Bolton W.	11.78	33	2	4
Brighton & H.A.	02.80	100	3	4
Leeds U.	12.82	5	0	0
Manchester C.	07.83	216	5	16
Tranmere Rov.	01.90	94	11	6
Huddersfield T.	01.92	11	0	0
Darlington	09.93	4	0	0

McSHANE, Henry (Harry)
Holytown, 8 April, 1920

Blackburn Rov.	04.37	2	0	0
Huddersfield T.	09.46	15	0	1
Bolton W.		93	0	6
Manchester U.	09.50	56	0	8
Oldham Ath.	02.54	41	0	5

MANNING, John Joseph
Liverpool, 11 December, 1940

Tranmere Rov.	05.62	130	0	70
Shrewsbury T.	10.66	39	0	18
Norwich C.	09.67	60	0	21
Bolton W.	03.69	27	2	7
Walsall	07.71	13	1	6
Tranmere Rov.	03.72	5	0	1
Crewe Alex.	08.72	37	1	9
Barnsley	09.73	41	4	7
Crewe Alex.	11.75	7	0	5

MARSH, Arthur
Dudley, 4 May, 1947

Bolton W.	05.65	71	2	0
Rochdale	12.71	89	1	0
Darlington	07.74	23	0	0

MATTHEWS, Neil
Grimsby, 19 September, 1966

Grimsby T.	09.84	9	2	1
Scunthorpe U.	11.85	1	0	0
Halifax T.	10.86	9	0	2
Bolton W.	03.87	1	0	0
Halifax T.	08.87	99	6	29
Stockport Co.	07.90	27	16	15
Halifax T.	09.91	3	0	0
Lincoln C.	12.92	52	8	18

MATHEWSON, Robert
Newcastle, 13 April, 1930

Bolton W.	03.48	3	0	0
Lincoln C.	06.53			

MAXWELL, Alistair
Hamilton, 29 June, 1960

Bolton W. (L)	03.92	3	0	0

Accepted wisdom on the soccer circuit was that Greaves' men would make up for their disappointment in 1976/77, and as the campaign drew towards a close they were poised for the top-three finish that would elevate them to the premier flight. But then came a home defeat by champions-elect Wolves and a draw at Bristol Rovers - and the Trotters had missed out by a single point for the second successive term.

It was bitter gall for the supporters, who had returned to Burnden Park in their droves, though there was some consolation in the club's best-ever run in the League Cup. They disposed of Bradford City, Fulham, Swansea City and Derby County on the way to a semi-final with Everton, which was lost 2-1 on aggregate.

To his eternal credit, Greaves did not panic, keeping faith with his players and finally reaping his just reward. In fact, the side that lifted the Second Division title in 1977/78 showed just one significant addition to that of the previous

term. The inimitable Frank Worthington arrived from Leicester City, adding variety and spice to the Wanderers attack, with a fair quota

of goals thrown in for good measure. In terms of entertainment alone, not to mention the little matter of that long-awaited trophy, the club record £90,000 needed to land Frank was money brilliantly spent. Bolton began the campaign as they meant to go on, recording three straight wins and not losing until their seventh game, which saw their only League defeat before December. A slight stutter around the

PETER THOMPSON
1973/74 - 1977/78

There is no substitute for class, a quality Peter Thompson had in abundance. Though he had spent his prime in the red shirt of Liverpool, helping Bill Shankly's men to lift two League Championships and an FA Cup, the Carlisle-born, right-footed left-winger was still a fabulous entertainer when he joined the Wanderers, initially on loan, in November 1973. At that time the country was reeling under the effects of a power strike and a three-day working week, and spirits were understandably low. Floodlit games were out, so Bolton's home encounter with Sunderland was played on a Wednesday afternoon. Some 8,000 souls, most of them in dire need of a lift, paid their entrance money and noted that Peter was making his Trotters debut. Many of them would have shaken their heads knowingly, thinking that here was a faded former star seeking a comfortable billet for his declining years. But two hours later, as they strode away from Burnden Park, they would have been telling a different tale, recalling the dancing feet of a soccer sorcerer whose appetite for the game was as keen as ever. That dismal afternoon, they had marvelled as Peter wrought havoc in the Wearsiders' defence and set up the winner for Neil Whatmore. Soon Trotters boss Jimmy Armfield had secured the England international's signature for £18,000 and given his side an exciting new attacking dimension. For two and a half terms, as Bolton consolidated in the Second Division and then set their sights on promotion, Peter was a regular and a favourite of the fans. True, he had slowed down since his Anfield heyday, but they loved him for his magical skills and for the fact that he wasn't there just for the ride. After 1976 came two seasons on the fringe of the side before he retired in 1978, aged 35, to run a hotel in the Lake District.

MAY, Andrew Michael Peter
Bury, 26 January, 196

Manchester C.	01.82	141	9	8
Huddersfield T.	07.87	112	2	5
Bolton W.	03.88	9	1	2
Bristol C.	08.90	88	2	4
Millwall	06.92	35	3	1

MIDDLEBROUGH, Alan
Rochdale, 4 December, 1925

Bolton W.	07.46	5	0	1
Bradford C.	08.48	4	0	0
Rochdale	10.48	47	0	25

MOIR, William
Aberdeen, 19 April, 1922   Died 1988

Bolton W.	04.43	325	0	118
Stockport Co.	09.55	69	0	26

MOORES, James Craig
Macclesfield, 1 February, 1961

Bolton W.	02.79	0	1	0
Swindon T.	07.81	1	1	0

MOORES, Ian Richard
Chesterton, 5 October, 1954

Stoke C.	06.72	40	10	14
Tottenham H.	08.76	25	4	6
Leyton Orient	10.78	110	7	26
Bolton W.	07.82	23	3	3
Barnsley	02.83	3	0	0

MORGAN, Trevor James
Forest Gate, 30 September, 1956

Bournemouth	09.80	53	0	13
Mansfield T.	11.81	12	0	6
Bournemouth	03.82	88	0	33
Bristol C.	03.84	32	0	8
Exeter C.	11.84	30	0	9
Bristol Rov.	09.85	54	1	24
Bristol C.	01.87	19	0	7
Bolton W.	06.87	65	12	17
Colchester U.	10.89	31	1	12
Exeter C.	11.90	14	3	3
Birmingham C. (N/C)	08.93	0	1	0

MORGAN, William (Willie)
Glasgow, 2 October, 1944

Burnley	10.61	183	0	19
Manchester U.	08.68	236	2	25
Burnley	06.75	12	1	0
Bolton W.	03.76	154	1	10
Blackpool	09.80	41	1	4

MOWBRAY, Henry
Hamilton, 1 May, 1947

Blackpool	05.67	88	3	0
Bolton W.	06.71	31	0	0

MULLINEUX, Ian J.
Salford, 10 November, 1968

Bolton W. (YT)	07.86	1	1	0

MURPHY, Daniel
Burtonwood, 10 May, 1922

Bolton W.	02.43	66	0	1
Crewe Alex.	01.52	106	0	1
Rochdale	07.54	109	0	0

turn of the year was righted by a run of eight outings without defeat and now there was a feeling of inevitability about their progress, although the late, late letdowns of previous years ensured against complacency.

Fourteen years in the wilderness ended in the season's penultimate game, a Worthington strike sealing victory at Blackburn and with it promotion. That set up an emotional last-day beano at Burnden Park, more than 34,000 fans turning up to see Bolton take the Second Division Championship for the first time since 1909. If the game, a goalless draw against mid-table Fulham, was something of an anti-climax, the occasion itself and what it meant to a proud club was quite the opposite.

Medals went to ever-present goalkeeper Jim McDonagh, defenders Sam Allardyce, Mike Walsh, Paul Jones, Peter Nicholson, John Ritson and Tony Dunne, midfielders Roy Greaves, Peter Reid and Ray Train, winger Willie Morgan - who had contributed royally since his arrival from Burnley in the spring of 1976 - and front-men Neil Whatmore and Frank Worthington. Ian Greaves' champions were not a spectacular side to watch, their goal count of 63 for and 33 against rather representing a study in efficiency that was a mirror of their manager's pragmatic approach. However, with gifted ball-players such as

SAM ALLARDYCE 1973/74 - 1979/80 and 1985/86

It was the day Sam Allardyce truly found a place in the hearts of the Burnden Park faithful. Just after Christmas 1975, Bolton were a goal down in the second half of a home clash with Second Division promotion rivals Sunderland and fears were mounting that a crucial game was slipping away. Then the Wanderers forced a corner and centre-half Sam trotted forward, but as the ball came across there seemed little danger as it dropped towards a trio of Wearside defenders on the edge of the box. Suddenly the big stopper exploded into action: diving between his startled markers, he powered a fearsome header into the net from 18 yards to set up a recovery which resulted in a stirring victory. Of course, the moustachioed West Midlander's principal responsibility was as a bulwark of the Trotters' rearguard and, during his 1970s prime, he fulfilled it efficiently and unfussily. A product of the club's youth side, in which he had excelled as a goal-scoring centre-half, he was kept waiting for a regular senior place behind Paul Jones and Don McAllister, but when the latter joined Spurs early in 1975, Sam was ready. Soon he had established his credentials, being particularly impressive in the air, and was a stalwart of the Second Division Championship side of 1977/78. However, after relegation in 1980 Sam accepted a £150,000 move to Sunderland, thereafter switching clubs regularly before rejoining Bolton from Huddersfield for £10,000 in July 1985. He was hampered by injuries, though, and never became re-established, soon moving on to Preston, then West Bromwich Albion, before becoming a youth coach at Deepdale. He broke into League management at the start of the 1994/95 season with Blackpool.

Morgan and Worthington in the side, they could - and often did - serve up attractive football.

Now came the difficult task of consolidation at the top level. Striker Alan Gowling, recruited from Newcastle United in March, proved an able foil for 'Worthy' and their double-act - with Frank scoring 24 and Alan 15 League goals - was to be the highlight of 1978/79. Meanwhile, ten weeks into the season, the Trotters forked out their first quarter-of-a-million-pound fee for Spurs' Neil McNab to bolster the midfield. But the defence lacked security, especially away from home, and ten of the first 17 games were lost.

However, it was very much a Jekyll-and-Hyde campaign, with sorry sequences being balanced by better ones, and it culminated in a 17th-place finish. In fact, but for a dreadful last month, in which Bolton garnered only three points from eight games, they would have achieved real respectability. In any case, with Chelsea and Birmingham City being well adrift from the pack, relegation was never a real threat.

That summer Greaves spent heavily on what he saw as urgent priorities, recruiting England right-back Dave Clement from Queen's Park Rangers and breaking the Trotters' transfer record yet again, paying West Bromwich Albion £350,000 for the stylish midfielder Len Cantello. Unluckily, injuries and illness limited the contribution of both newcomers and after taking four points out of six in their first three games - including an admirable draw at Anfield - they did not register another League victory until March.

By then Ian Greaves had been sacked (in

81

January, two days after Bolton beat Halifax Town to reach the fifth round of the FA Cup), his heady achievement of 20 months earlier failing to stand him in good stead when the

chips were down. Promoted in his place was assistant boss Stan Anderson, a man of experience who had managed Middlebrough, AEK Athens and Doncaster Rovers in his

TONY DUNNE
1973/74 - 1978/79

When Tommy Docherty allowed Tony Dunne to leave Old Trafford and join Bolton on a free transfer in August 1973, few at Burnden Park realised what an outsize favour Manchester United were conferring on the Wanderers. Obviously The Doc would not have agreed, but at the time many shrewd judges reckoned 32-year-old Tony was still the best full-back on the books of the relegation-bound Reds. Most Bolton fans, while welcoming such a classy operator, did not expect more than a couple of years' service, at best, and they feared that might be at half-throttle. How wrong they were! Soon the undemonstrative Republic of Ireland international was showing that he had lost little of his searing pace and none of his waspishness in the tackle or skill on the ball; and as a bonus, now he was not in such stellar company, he was more inclined to be ambitious in his distribution and sprint forward tellingly into attack. Most remarkable of all, though, was that Tony just kept on going. He was still there in '76 and '77 when Bolton narrowly missed out on promotion to the top flight, still there when they won the Second Division title in '78, still there when they took their place among the elite the following season. By the time he finally retired in 1979 - soon after doing his usual unspectacular but efficient job in an oh-so-sweet victory at Old Trafford - he was close to his 38th birthday. The following year he was back at Burnden, first as a coach and then as assistant boss to Stan Anderson, leaving when he was replaced by George Mulhall in the spring of 1981. Tony will be remembered as one of Ian Greaves' finest signings, and that's high praise, indeed.

NAPIER, Robert John
Lurgan (NI), 23 September, 1946

Bolton W.	09.63	69	0	2
Brighton & H.A.	08.67	218	1	5
Bradford C.	10.72	106	1	3

NEAL, Philip George
Irchester, 29 February, 1951

Northampton T.	12.68	182	4	29
Liverpool	10.74	453	2	41
Bolton W.	12.85	56	8	3

NEILL, Thomas Kerr
Methil, 3 October, 1930

Bolton W.	09.50	40	0	2
Bury	12.56	90	0	9
Tranmere Rov.	10.60	79	0	2

NICHOLSON, Peter
Cleator Moor, 12 January, 1951

Blackpool	08.69	3	3	0
Bolton W.	06.71	303	15	12
Rochdale (N/C)	11.82	7	0	0
Carlisle U. (N/C)	03.83	1	2	0

NIKOLIC, Dusan
Yugoslavia, 23 January, 1953

Bolton W.	10.80	22	0	2

NOWAK, Tadeusz
Poland, 28 November, 1948

Bolton W.	03.79	22	2	1

OGHANI, George William
Manchester, 2 September, 1960

Bury	02.78			
Bolton W.	10.83	86	13	27
Wrexham	03.87	6	1	0
Burnley	06.87	73	1	21
Stockport Co.	06.89	5	3	2
Hereford U.	10.89	7	1	2
Scarborough	02.90	43	7	18
Carlisle U.	08.92	45	8	15

OLINYK, Peter
Bolton, 4 October, 1953

Bolton W.	06.71	7	3	0
Stockport Co.	11.74	4	0	0

OLIVER, Darren
Liverpool, 1 November, 1971

Bolton W.	05.90	3	0	0
Rochdale	10.93	14	5	0

OXTOBY, Richard
Chesterfield, 5 September, 1939

Bolton W.	01.57	3	0	0
Tranmere Rov.	07.63	5	0	0

PARKINSON, Gary Anthony
Thorneby, 10 January, 1968

Middlesbrough	01.86	194	8	5
Southend U.	10.92	6	0	0
Bolton W.	03.93	1	2	0
Burnley	01.94	20	0	1

time, but who now faced an impossible task in averting the drop when only 11 points had been gained from 24 games. Nevertheless, under new leadership the Wanderers improved slightly, losing eight, drawing six and winning four of their final 18 matches, the victories including a famous one over European Cup holders Nottingham Forest at Burnden Park thanks to a lone goal from Whatmore. Of course, it was not enough to lift them from bottom spot and they would have needed 11 more points to survive. Though the worst had happened, there was a feeling that Bolton would make a good showing in 1980/81, especially with the arrival of forward reinforcements such as the well-travelled Brian Kidd from Everton and a talented but little-known Yugoslavian international, Dusan Nikolic from Red Star Belgrade. But the script went drastically wrong,

PETER REID 1974/75 - 1982/83

'If only . . .' Two of the most oft-repeated words in football, and poignantly apposite when applied to the happy-sad association of Bolton Wanderers and Peter Reid. The pugnacious, strong-willed little Lancastrian was not the most extravagantly gifted midfielder to grace Burnden Park since the war, but there is little doubt - in view of his later achievements at Everton - that he possessed the potential to be the most influential. As it was, Peter didn't do badly. As a teenager in 1974/75, he became established and helped Ian Greaves' side to consolidate in the Second Division; then followed two seasons in which he was ever-present, and in which Bolton were only just pipped for promotion; finally came triumph in the shape of the Championship in 1977/78, when his emergence as a major talent was confirmed by England under-21 honours. Throughout this period, he was one of the most crucial cogs in the Trotters' machine. Though never quick, he made up for it with deceptively simple yet perceptive distribution, a nagging knack of nicking the ball away from opponents when they least expected it and, most important of all, an irrepressible vitality that rubbed off on his colleagues. But then, just as the club and Peter might have been poised for a great future together, the dreaded 'if only' syndrome took over. A grisly combination of horrendous injuries - including two broken legs, torn knee ligaments and cartilage trouble - and contractural disputes meant that for each of the next five seasons Peter appeared in only about one-third of senior games. His input was sorely missed over two terms of top-flight travail and it seemed that after Everton, Arsenal and Wolves had each bid £600,000 for him after Bolton's 1980 relegation, he would be on his way. But both fitness and financial problems persisted, and it was not until December 1982 that he moved to Goodison at a tenth of the initial valuation. After a disappointing start at Goodison, he matured into one of England's most effective play-makers, reaping a rich harvest of club honours and winning 13 England caps. Later, Peter took his fearless, hard-working approach into management at Manchester City, showing considerable promise before he was sacked, harshly in the estimation of most neutral observers. However, it would have been surprising if football has seen the last of Peter Reid and since then he has played with Notts County during the 1993/94 season before registering with Bury.

PARRY, Raymond Alan
Derby, 19 January, 1936

Bolton W.	01.53	270	0	68
Blackpool	10.60	128	0	27
Bury	10.64	136	10	17

PATTERSON, Mark Andrew
Darwen, 24 May, 1965

Blackburn Rov.	05.83	89	12	20
Preston N. E.	06.88	54	1	19
Bury	02.90	42	0	10
Bolton W.	01.90	123	4	7

PEACOCK, Dennis
Lincoln, 19 April, 1953

Nottingham F.	04.71	22	0	0
Walsall	03.73	10	0	0
Doncaster Rov.	07.75	199	0	0
Bolton W.	03.80	16	0	0
Doncaster Rov.	08.82	130	0	0
Burnley	09.85	8	0	0

PEYTON, Gerald Joseph
Birmingham, 20 May, 1956

Burnley	05.75	30	0	0
Fulham	12.76	345	0	0
Southend U.	09.83	10	0	0
Bournemouth	07.86	202	0	0
Everton	07.91			
Bolton W.	02.92	1	0	0
Brentford	09.92	14	0	0
Chelsea	01.93	0	1	0
Brentford	03.93	5	0	0
West Ham U.	06.93			

PHILLIPS, James Neil
Bolton, 8 February, 1966

Bolton W.	08.83	103	5	2
Oxford U.	08.88	79	0	6
Middlesbrough	03.90	139	0	6
Bolton W.	07.93	41	1	0

PHILLIPS, Ronald Daniel
Worsley, 30 March, 1947

Bolton W.	10.65	135	10	17
Chesterfield	01.75	5	0	0
Bury	06.75	68	4	5
Chester C.	09.77	128	2	21

PHILLISKIRK, Anthony
Sunderland, 10 February, 1965

Sheffield U.	08.83	62	18	20
Rotherham U.	10.86	6	0	1
Oldham Ath.	07.88	3	7	1
Preston N. E.	02.89	13	1	6
Bolton W.	06.89	139	2	52
Peterborough U.	10.92	37	6	15
Burnley	01.94	19	0	7

PHYTHIAN, Ernest Rixon
Farnworth, 16 July, 1942

Bolton W.	07.59	10	0	3
Wrexham	03.62	134	0	44
Hartlepool U.	06.65	124	0	50

PIKE, Martin Russell
South Shields, 21 October, 1964

West Bromwich A.	10.82	

with many old favourites - including Roy Greaves, Worthington and Morgan - departing and a dismal sequence of results that lengthened steadily. Though the goal tallies of Kidd, Whatmore and Gowling all reached double figures, the defence was leaky, and a distinctly shaky 18th place was the result.

It was a campaign of few pluses - the highest note being struck by a spirited 3-3 draw at Nottingham Forest in the FA Cup - and, predictably enough, Anderson was axed in May. Into his seat moved George Mulhall, who had coached at Bolton under Ian Greaves, then managed Bradford City, before returning to Burnden and helping to produce a slight upturn in results as Stan's assistant in March. The brief now facing him, however, was not an enviable one.

Not surprisingly, attendances had tumbled once more and Bolton's financial resources were seriously depleted. As one of his first acts, Mulhall had no choice but to sell the excellent

Whatmore to Birmingham City for £340,000 - which remained the record fee received by Boltonuntil the departure of Andy Walker in 1994 - and other players were released to reduce the

wage bill. With morale dangerously low, the first 11 League games brought nine defeats and a season-long battle for survival had begun. It was won, though with only two points to spare, and when the board

embarked on further cost-cutting in the summer of 1982, Mulhall took issue with some of their suggestions and departed in frustration. Once more this great club was on the skids,

and the downward plunge gathered pace alarmingly in 1982/83. The new hand on the tiller was that of John McGovern, the club's first player-boss. Fresh from a distinguished playing career of which

Peterborough U.	08.83	119	7	8
Sheffield U.	08.86	127	2	5
Tranmere Rov.	11.89	2	0	0
Bolton W.	12.89	5	0	1
Fulham	02.90	187	3	14

PILKINGTON, Brian
Leyland, 12 February, 1933

Burnley	04.51	300	0	67
Bolton W.	03.61	82	0	11
Bury	02.64	19	0	0
Barrow	02.65	86	1	9

PILLING, Vincent
Bolton, 8 January, 1932

Bolton W.	10.52	7	0	0
Bradford P. A.	08.55	9	0	1

PLATT, John Roger
Ashton0u0Lyne, 22 August, 1954

Oldham Ath.	06.72	109	0	0
Bury	08.81	20	0	0
Bolton W.	07.83	10	0	0
Tranmere Rov.	11.84	8	0	0
Preston N. E.	02.85	38	0	0

POOLE, Terence
Chesterfield, 16 December, 1949

Manchester U.	02.67			
Huddersfield T.	08.68	207	0	0
Bolton W.	01.77	29	0	0
Sheffield U.	03.80	7	0	0

REDFEARN, Neil David
Dewsbury, 20 June, 1965

Bolton W.	06.82	35	0	1
Lincoln C.	03.84	96	4	13
Doncaster Rov.	08.86	46	0	14
Crystal Palace	07.87	57	0	10
Watford	11.88	22	2	3
Oldham Ath.	01.90	56	6	16
Barnsley	09.91	127	1	19

REDFERN, James
Kirkby, 1 August, 1952

Bolton W.	08.69	19	5	2
Chester C.	08.73	98	8	15

REDROBE, William Eric
Wigan, 23 August, 1944

Bolton W.	02.62	4	0	1
Southport	08.66	186	6	55
Hereford U.	10.72	75	12	17

REEVES, David
Birkenhead, 19 November, 1967

Sheffield Wed.	08.86	8	9	2
Scunthorpe U.	12.86	3	1	2
Scunthorpe U.	10.87	6	0	4
Burnley	11.87	16	0	8
Bolton W.	08.89	111	23	30
Notts Co.	03.93	9	4	2
Carlisle U.	10.93	34	0	11

REID, Peter
Huyton, 20 June, 1956

Bolton W.	05.74	222	3	23
Everton	12.82	155	4	8

MIKE WALSH
1974/75 - 1980/81

Mike Walsh was a versatile member of one of the meanest defensive barriers ever erected at Burnden Park - and that's saying something! The big, blond Mancunian was at his best at centre-half, but also did a fair job at left-back, notably deputising when Tony Dunne was injured during the mid-1970s. At that time Paul Jones and Sam Allardyce were established at the heart of the rearguard, but when injury to Paul prevented him from starting 1977/78, it was Mike's moment to shine. Slotting in alongside Sam, he was dominant in the air and sensible on the ground, and he became an integral part of the side that won the Second Division title. The Walsh standard did not slip in the top flight, despite the Trotters coming under consistently heavy defensive pressure, and it was no surprise when several big clubs began to monitor his progress. Accordingly in August 1981, a year after relegation, Mike moved to Everton in exchange for £90,000 and goalkeeper Jim McDonagh, who was making the return journey to Burnden. However, his chances were limited during a period of sweeping change at Goodison and after two in-and-out seasons - during which he won Eire caps, courtesy of his ancestry - he crossed the Atlantic to Fort Lauderdale Strikers. There followed a brief fling with Manchester City before the strapping stopper gave five years' solid service to Blackpool, then managed Bury. Oddly for a man whose main job was stopping goals, he remains best remembered at Burnden for a rare one he scored, a 30-yard left-footer to equalise against Fulham in stoppage time of a League Cup tie in October 1976.

87

the climax had been captaining Nottingham Forest to two European Cup triumphs, he found himself in starkly contrasting circumstances. With no managerial experience and little money to supplement a squad of indifferent quality, he was up against it from the first.

Though fiercely dedicated to his job, McGovern could not prevent Bolton from propping up the Second Division at the end of a dispiriting season. The board stood by him for 1983/84, and though they were not repaid by promotion, John did at least espouse an attractive attacking style of which his mentor, Brian Clough, would have approved. His young team finished tenth in the Third Division and he approached 1984/85 with a spring in his step.

Sadly, by the New Year the Trotters were wallowing in the nether regions of the table and, after two-and-a-half years of honest toil, McGovern was replaced by chief coach Charlie Wright, whose goalkeeping exploits had

helped Bolton win the Third Division title in 1973. While still in temporary charge, the extrovert Glaswegian presided over four successive League wins - with front-man Tony Caldwell hitting the mark in each one - but as soon as he was confirmed in the post, the side embarked on an horrendous sequence which brought only one point out of a possible

WILLIE MORGAN
1975/76 - 1979/80

To people who didn't know the man, the end seemed to be in sight for Willie Morgan when he arrived at Burnden Park in March 1976. It wasn't just that he was presumed to have left his best days behind him at Old Trafford; since then he had spent an unproductive few months at Burnley and had been released to join Bolton on a free transfer. Surely, went the theory, the 31-year-old was being put out to grass and the Trotters were daft enough to pay for his keep. However, such glib judgements could not have been more wrong. Willie, a proud and richly talented individual, exerted a mammoth influence on his new club's midfield, remaining in the team until the turn of the decade. During that time he helped them win the Second Division Championship in 1977/78 and then complete a sweet and well-deserved League double over the Red Devils during the first term back among the elite. During this period, Willie surprised many by his sheer consistency. His days of being a wonder winger were gone along with his pace, but now he allied his still-superb technique to hard-won experience. Invariably he selected the correct option for his crosses and passes, and delivered them with impeccable accuracy. His spirit, too, was invaluable to the cause and it dawned gradually on the delighted supporters that he was one of the shrewdest signings of Ian Greaves' managerial reign. Sadly, Willie was part of a side doomed to relegation in 1979/80, though he was replaced by Tadeusz Nowak for the last three months of the campaign and was not present at the death. The following September, a month short of his 36th birthday, he moved to Blackpool via Minnesota Kicks to end his career.

27. The ship was steadied in time to prevent the ultimate disaster of sinking to the League's basement, but the end-of-term 17th spot satisfied no-one at Burnden Park.

Wright concluded that experienced heads were needed to bolster all areas of the team. Accordingly, former Bolton stalwart Sam Allardyce and his fellow stopper Dave Sutton were drafted in from Huddersfield Town, the veteran but still effective midfielder Asa Hartford arrived from Norwich City and seasoned target man David Cross was signed from West Bromwich Albion. But results were chronic and Wright departed in December to be replaced, as a one-match caretaker, by Nat Lofthouse (who else?) before former Liverpool and England full-back Phil Neal picked up the gauntlet.

Neal, operating as a player-boss, improved matters enough to stave off relegation and, a considerable bonus, led the Trotters to Wembley for the final of the Freight Rover Trophy. Though they lost 3-0 to Bristol City, Bolton's first trip to the Twin Towers for 28 years lifted the spirits of fans, players and officials alike and the line-up that day deserves to be recorded. It comprised Simon Farnworth in goal, defenders Derek Scott, Jimmy Phillips, Dave Sutton, Mark Came and Phil Neal, midfielders Asa Hartford (captain), Steve Thompson and

substitute Graham Bell, and forwards Mark Gavin, Tony Caldwell and George Oghani.

After such adventures, few thought Bolton would be involved in the relegation scrap in

1986/87 but they were and - horror of horrors - they sank to the Fourth Division for the first time. The end came via play-off defeat against Aldershot, who consigned one of

ALAN GOWLING
1977/78 - 1981/82

Alan Gowling was an ugly duckling of a footballer. Tall, gangling and lacking the slightest degree of grace in his movement, he was in his element when ploughing through a morass of stamina-sapping mud or scrapping energetically for a loose ball when the efforts of more elegant colleagues had come to nought. But what a mightily effective operator he could be, particularly during his Bolton heyday alongside Frank Worthington in 1978/79. Together the vividly contrasting pair - Frank was as languidly cultured as Alan was heartily rumbustious - were the scourge of First Division defences as Wanderers sought to consolidate their newly-regained top-flight status. Gowling had begun his career with Manchester United, achieving modest success as a striker before moving to midfield, but then reverted to the front line in spells at Huddersfield and Newcastle. He left St James' Park for Burnden in March 1978 in a £120,000 deal that was a record for Bolton at the time, and made a handful of appearances as the Second Division championship was secured. Then came that wonderful interlude alongside 'Worthy' - Alan netted 16 times in his first full season as a Trotter - but after his partner left, he struggled for goals and Wanderers were relegated. By now he was a target for criticism by his home crowd, but he battled away in the Second, never prolific but contributing his share of bread-and-butter goals. As the side continued to struggle in 1981/82, he switched to central defence and did a solid job alongside Paul Jones, his strength and bravery standing him in admirable stead. Alan, an articulate economics graduate who served a term as PFA chairman and later enjoyed a successful business career, left in 1982 to end his playing days at Preston.

soccer's most famous names to the bottom flight after extra time in the second leg at Burnden. A mere four League wins after Christmas told a sorry story and many thought

Neal would be shown the exit, especially after he had ruffled many feathers with comments denigrating the situation he had inherited at Bolton.

But the board believed in him and their level-headed approach was rewarded with success in 1987/88. Neal had opted for selective but incisive surgery to his side, the most notable newcomers being a former Trotter, striker John Thomas, from Preston and midfielder Robbie Savage from Bradford City, each at a cost of £30,000. Both were major forces in securing the third automatic promotion place, Thomas netting 22 times and Savage scoring the crucial winner in the final match at Wrexham.

The leading lights in Bolton's rise were 'keeper David Felgate, defenders Scott, Sutton, Came and Dean Crombie, midfielders Savage, Thompson, Julian Darby and Nicky Brookman, and forwards Thomas, Trevor Morgan, Steve Elliott and Gary Henshaw.

At last the Wanderers appeared to be on the road to full recovery. The following term Neal, abetted by able coach Mick Brown, led them to a solid 10th place in Division Three after a worrying first half of the season, but the sweetest moment was delayed

until May 28 when Bolton returned to Wembley to collect their first trophy for 11 years. They won the renamed Sherpa Van Trophy, coming from behind to trounce Torquay United 4-1, with strikes from Darby, Crombie and Morgan supplemented by an own-goal by the West Countrymen's John Morrison. It was a glorious day for fans who had remained loyal through a series of traumas, aching for something to celebrate.

JIM McDONAGH 1976/77 - 1982/83

If long-time Wanderers fans were asked to draw up a top ten of the club's post-war goalkeepers - and though comparisons are invidious, they are irresistible - it is probable that Jim McDonagh would appear at number two in the majority of lists. Though few would reckon the Yorkshire-born Republic of Ireland international the equal of Eddie Hopkinson, it is difficult to see who would challenge him for the runners-up spot. The muscular six-footer joined Bolton (initially on loan) from Rotherham, his hometown club, in August 1976, just ahead of Barry Siddall's departure to Sunderland. Thereafter Jim didn't miss a game for the remainder of that term and was ever-present in 1977/78 as the Trotters took the Second Division title. Throughout that memorable season, he was a paragon of all-round reliability, being beaten only 33 times in the League, a club record for a 42-match programme. Jim didn't miss a match in the two top-flight campaigns that followed, either, performing well enough to earn a £250,000 move to Everton when Bolton went down in 1980. At Goodison he proved competent, but young Neville Southall was on the rise and in August 1981 Jim returned to Burnden as a makeweight in the deal that saw Mike Walsh join the Blues. For two years he did little wrong, but was caught up in another demotion in 1983 - one personal highlight was scoring with a long kick against Burnley in the January - after which he departed to Notts County. The amiable Jim, who positively revelled in the Irishness conferred on him by ancestry rather than birth, was nicknamed 'Seamus' after winning the first of his 24 caps, and is still recalled with affection in Bolton. Later he played in the USA and for six more English clubs before managing Galway United.

The men who obliged were Felgate; Phil Brown, Crombie, Mark Winstanley, Barry Cowdrill; Savage, Thompson, Darby; Jeff Chandler (substitute Stuart Storer), Morgan and Thomas.
The 1989/90 campaign signalled continued progress. Strengthened by the arrival of a new strike-force - Preston's prolific Tony Philliskirk and David Reeves from Sheffield Wednesday - and the addition of Burnley midfielder Paul

JEFF CHANDLER 1981/82 - 1984/85 and 1987/88 -1989/90

Jeff Chandler was a gifted but frequently frustrating footballer. Versatile enough to play on either midfield flank or in the centre or even up front, he could both make and take chances, and at his best looked a high-quality player. But, and it was quite a sizeable but, the overall Chandler contribution was marred by inconsistency and a propensity for drifting on the edge of the action. London-born Jeff had shone with his first club, Blackpool, and appeared to have achieved his big breakthrough when a £100,000 deal took him to Leeds in September 1979. However, the Elland Road scene was turbulent at the time and despite winning two caps for the Republic of Ireland, he did not settle, crossing the Pennines to Burnden Park for £40,000 in October 1981. He became a regular, went down with the Wanderers in 1982/83, then remained an important member of the team as he scored 37 senior goals over the next two campaigns. That prompted Derby County to sign him for £38,000 (a tribunal valuation) in the summer of 1985, and he helped the Rams gain promotion to the Second in his first term. Still, though, Jeff had itchy feet and in July 1987 they took him back to Bolton, this time at a cost of £20,000. Sadly, injury cost him all but three appearances in the promotion campaign that followed and in 1988/89 he was in and out of the side. He did secure a Wembley winner's medal, though, helping to beat Torquay in the Sherpa Van Trophy Final. He claimed a goal, too, but it was rubbed out by the statisticians, who had no alternative but to count his deflected shot as an own goal by United's John Morrison. Jeff joined Cardiff in November 1989 before leaving League football.

93

FRANK WORTHINGTON
1977/78 - 1979/80

A prodigiously talented footballer and
outrageously extrovert character, Frank
Worthington brought excitement and colour to any
club he was with - and he was with rather a lot in
his time. Indeed, in the Football League alone
there were 11, of which Bolton was his third.
Frank arrived at Burnden Park in September 1977,
aged 28 and probably at his creative peak, and he
won the fans' hearts with two years of captivating
entertainment. He had a reputation as a rebel, but
Trotters boss Ian Greaves knew him well, having
managed him at Huddersfield and, after seeing
how he bedded in during a short loan period, had
no qualms about writing Leicester a £90,000
cheque for his signature. In bare statistics - and
really that's not the way to recall 'Worthy' - he
was fabulously successful, his 11 goals helping
Bolton take the Second Division title in 1978, then
a further 24 going a massive way towards
preventing an immediate exit from the top flight.
In fact, in that 1978/79 season he topped the First
Division scoring charts, leaving a certain Kenny
Dalglish trailing in second place - enough said!
But what sums up Frank best of all are the
memories of two special goals. For the first one, at
Loftus Road in December 1978, he went past two
defenders inside the centre-circle, then, seeing Phil
Parkes off his line, he chipped him from just inside
the Queen's Park Rangers half. The second, at
home to Ipswich the following April, was even
more astounding. Surrounded by a posse of
opponents who were determined to deny him the
slightest glimmer of an opening, he took
possession on the edge of the box, mesmerised his
markers by flicking the ball up twice, then ran
round them to thrash it into the net. It was the sort
of trick even Roy of the Rovers might have
thought twice about attempting, but to Frank it was
second nature. Sadly, Bolton could not hog such an
inveterate bird of passage indefinitely and in
October 1980, after a summer in the North
American League which seemed to take a lot out
of him, he joined Birmingham for £150,000. It was
sad to see him go, but better to have loved and

STEVE THOMPSON
1982/83 - 1991/92

Steve Thompson was the outstanding player in the Bolton side which reeled from crisis to crisis in the 1980s before winning promotion from the Fourth Division in 1988. The dynamic midfielder will be remembered also as a central figure in the Trotters' two trips to Wembley, for the Freight Rover defeat by Bristol City in 1986 and the glorious return to beat Torquay United in the Sherpa Van Trophy three years later. Steve, whose father Jim was a wing-half with four League clubs in the 1950s and 1960s, impressed in a strong Wanderers youth side before making his senior debut at Derby in November 1982. But it was not until the following season, after demotion to the Third, that he began to make his mark with his blend of skill and power. Gradually Steve grew ever more influential, contributing more goals as his confidence mushroomed, being especially dangerous from long distance and from dead-ball situations. By the turn of the decade, the Oldham-born mixture of graft and craft had matured into a highly saleable asset and transfer rumours circulated constantly. The inevitable happened in August 1991 when the 26-year-old departed to Luton in a £200,000 deal. However, Kenilworth Road proved a brief billet and, after less than two months, he switched to Leicester. At Filbert Street, Steve came into his own, featuring in three consecutive efforts to reach the top flight, finally succeeding in 1994.

Comstive, the Trotters came sixth in the table, despite winning only one of their last eight games. That earned them a play-off spot but they could not overcome Notts County, a just outcome as the Magpies had finished no less than 18 points above them. Knockout competition had produced excitement, too, especially a League Cup marathon with Swindon Town, which Bolton shaded after four games, and a run to the northern semi-final of the (renamed again) Leyland Daf Trophy. By now Phil Neal was

TONY CALDWELL 1983/84 - 1986/87

Tony Caldwell was, in footballing terms, 'The Man From Nowhere'. Like some taciturn stranger in a cowboy film, he blew into Burnden Park, virtually unknown to anyone - but within a very short time, he was the talk of the town. In fact, 25-year-old Tony had been a part-time electrician who had been scoring prolifically for Northern Premier League side Horwich RMI. Trotters boss John McGovern took him on a pre-1983/84 tour of Ireland and he impressed sufficiently to win a place in the side that kicked off the Third Division campaign. On his second League outing, the fleet-footed marksman scored in a win at Bradford City, but it was in his fourth game that he made the offer of a full-time contract a formality. At home to Walsall, Tony ran riot, scoring five times in the sort of dream performance that most strikers do not experience during a whole career. Of course, he could not be expected to reach such heights again - and he didn't - but over four years as a Wanderer he more than justified his £2,000 elevation from the non-League ranks, finishing each term as the club's top scorer. In addition, his goal in each leg of the 1986 Freight Rover Trophy semi-final against Wigan saw Bolton reach Wembley, though he could not prevent relegation to the Fourth Division in 1987. After that Tony joined Bristol City for £27,500 - the fee, decided by a transfer tribunal, seemed barely adequate for a regular scorer - but neither at Ashton Gate nor with three subsequent clubs did he approach his Burnden form.

being spoken of as one of *the* young managers to watch, and he did his reputation no harm in 1990/91, improving Bolton's position to fourth and missing automatic promotion by the excruciating margin of goal difference. This time they reached the play-off final at Wembley, but lost to Tranmere Rovers through the only goal of the match in extra time. What really rubbed in the frustration was that they had gathered five more points than the Wirral club during the season.

JIMMY PHILLIPS 1983/84 - 1986/87 and 1993/94 -

Jimmy Phillips, the only Bolton-born member of Bruce Rioch's exciting class of '94, is an attacking left-back whose powerful style is distinctly reminiscent of Stuart Pearce. And while a direct comparison with the former England captain may seem fanciful, the Trotters' blond six-footer had improved enormously as the first season of his second spell at Burnden drew to a close. Jimmy, who left school with ten O-levels to his credit, began his career with his hometown club. He made a fleeting appearance as a substitute in the spring of 1984, then replaced Ray Deakin at number three and retained the berth for the next three campaigns. Come March 1987, many were surprised when mighty Glasgow Rangers took the forceful 21-year-old for £75,000, and threw him into European Cup action the following autumn. Jimmy didn't forge a future at Ibrox, however, and he re-crossed the border to join Oxford United, then Middlesbrough, before returning to Bolton for £300,000 in the summer of 1993. Steady at the back and ambitious going forward, utilising the skills he had honed as a teenage midfielder, he was ideal for the constructive, forward-looking side Bruce Rioch was out to create. However, Jimmy took a few months to settle and there were raised eyebrows over his pre-Christmas form. But the New Year brought better displays and ever-increasing confidence, and he was so impressive on the FA Cup run that by May there were rumours linking him with Premiership clubs. That left Wanderers fans to hope that, this time around, Bolton could hold on to their own. If they do reach the top level in 1994/95 - and that seemed a realistic aim - Jimmy Phillips is just the type of player they will need.

JULIAN DARBY
1985/86 - 1992/93

Football fans can be both cruel and short-sighted, and sometimes their club can suffer as a result. Consider the case of Julian Darby, a Boltonian through and through who had made his senior Trotters debut as an 18-year-old and went on to play in every outfield position. During 1991/92, when the expected surge towards promotion from the Third Division never quite materialised, he suffered an uncharacteristic lapse in form. Instead of offering support, a vociferous element in the Burnden crowd vilified him continuously, making him a scapegoat for the overall failure of the team. There was off-the-pitch abuse, too, and in the end there was no alternative but for Julian to depart. It spoke volumes for his ability that the man who came in for him was his former manager at Bolton, Phil Neal, who took the supremely versatile 26-year-old to top-flight Coventry for £150,000 in the summer of 1993. Phil knew all about Julian's achievements, how he had made his debut in defence, then pulled his weight in a succession of roles before delivering arguably his best form in central midfield. Though he went down with Wanderers in '87, he played a major role in helping them bounce back to the Third at the first attempt and remained a valuable operator until the day he left. A veritable workaholic who tackled crisply and was not short of skill, he also packed a considerable shot. Indeed, his menace in front of goal was illustrated vividly in the spring of '94 when he struck twice for Coventry to beat Blackburn, thus confirming Manchester United as League Champions. And if that was not calculated to endear himself to Bolton followers, they have only themselves to blame.

The Burnden Park faithful could hardly wait for the new term in which, they firmly believed, nothing could stop their ascent. But somehow the impetus had gone and although there were only four League defeats before Christmas, form evaporated distressingly in the spring and, after dreaming of reaching the Second Division, they finished 13th in the Third. They performed creditably in the FA Cup, though, fighting through to the fifth round before losing to Southampton after a replay.

DAVID FELGATE 1985/86 - 1991/92

Goalkeeper David Felgate made a success of life with Bolton Wanderers the second time around. The tall Welshman graduated through the youth system at Burnden Park but was unable to achieve a senior breakthrough with the club, instead garnering League experience on loan with Rochdale and Crewe Alexandra in the late 1970s. By the dawn of the new decade, even with the temporary departure of Jim McDonagh to Everton, it was obvious that David's future lay away from Bolton, and in September 1980 a £25,000 deal took him to Lincoln City. He prospered as a Red Imp, winning his sole Welsh cap during his Sincil Bank tenure, then joined Grimsby before returning to the Trotters for two loan periods, first in February 1986 and then again a year later. Soon a £15,000 fee made the arrangement permanent and David was launched on the most successful phase of his career. Back in the Burnden fold, he shared the trauma of relegation to the Fourth Division in 1986/87, helped secure instant promotion the following term - he was voted the club's player of the year for his efforts - and played an important part in the Sherpa Van Trophy triumph of 1989. An agile shot-stopper who, in common with so many custodians, was not quite so consistent at dealing with crosses, David continued as first choice between the Bolton posts until 1992, when he was supplanted by Keith Branagan. He joined Chester for 1993/94, helping them rise from the Third Division.

The League letdown notwithstanding, in view of his progress over six and a half years at the club, Neal was not expected to lose his job. But come May 1992, he was unemployed and former Millwall boss Bruce Rioch was sitting in his office.

However keen many felt the injustice to be, it was hard to argue with the board's decision after a memorable 1992/93 campaign. After enduring a spell of five defeats in six League outings during the autumn, prospects of departing the new

ASA HARTFORD 1985/86 - 1986/87

Asa Hartford was nearing the end of an illustrious and eventful career when he joined Bolton in August 1985, but it was clear from the outset that the dynamic little midfielder had no intention of merely marking time until retirement. Trotters boss Charlie Wright, who had acquired the 34-year-old Scottish international on a free transfer from Norwich, lost little time in making him captain and he was an ever-present that term as relegation was narrowly averted. Operating as the side's creative hub and chief motivator, he worked diligently, raising the spirits of those around him. His skill and experience compensated amply for a natural loss of speed, and he richly deserved the player-of-the-year accolade bestowed on him by supporters. By way of relief from the grim facts of League life, Bolton reached Wembley to face Torquay in the Freight Rover Trophy Final and it was hoped that Asa's vast experience might nudge the result Wanderers' way. Sadly they lost 3-0, though optimists believed that he would inspire better things in 1986/87. Alas, the former West Bromwich Albion, Manchester City, Nottingham Forest and Everton star was declining in influence and Bolton were relegated to the League basement. There seemed little more Asa could offer the Bolton cause and in May 1987 he was released to become player-manager of Stockport County. Thereafter he went on to serve Oldham and Shrewsbury, delaying retirement until 1990 when he was only a few months short of his 40th birthday. How ironic to reflect that, some two decades earlier, his career was placed in apparent jeopardy - and a move to Don Revie's Leeds United scuppered - by a hole-in-the-heart condition. After a spell as reserve coach at Blackburn, he became assistant manager at Stoke City.

Second Division from the right end were beginning to look bleak and there were ominous rumblings from stand and terrace. But then came an unbeaten run of ten games to the year's end, and a magnificent sequence of only one reverse in 19 matches to complete the season as runners-up to Stoke City.

As if this bread-and-butter success wasn't ample, there was delicious jam in the FA Cup, in which Bolton unseated the holders, mighty Liverpool, in the third round. Unarguably

PHIL BROWN 1988/89 - 1993/94

As might be expected of a man who wore the number-two shirt so long and so successfully for his country, Phil Neal was a fine judge of a full-back, a fact never more in evidence than when he acquired the services of Phil Brown for £17,500 in June 1988. The genial north-easterner, 29 at the time, had spent his career to date in the lower divisions, first with Hartlepool United, then Halifax Town, yet had always been an enterprising performer. Indeed with Halifax, whom he had captained, Phil had scored 14 times during one campaign - remarkable for a full-back - and figured regularly in the PFA end-of-season 'best in the division' line-ups. Neal, who had been impressed by Brown's display in a cup encounter with the Shaymen, wasted little time in handing him the skipper's armband and he emerged as an outstanding organiser, both on and off the pitch. Phil led Bolton to triumph in the Sherpa Van Trophy at Wembley in 1989, through two disappointments in the Third Division promotion play-offs and, best of all, to second place in the new Second Division in 1992/93. Best of all? Well, some romantics would contend that such an accolade should be reserved for the 1993/94 FA Cup run, in which Phil belied his 34 years with a series of uplifting displays. He might not have been the fastest, but he was one of the canniest, and if his team-mates dubbed him the oldest swinger in town, it didn't bother him one bit! At the end of that season, Phil was given a free transfer and could leave Burnden in the knowledge of a job well done. A new career in coaching or management seemed a likely option. He started 1994/95 at Blackpool under Sam Allardyce.

it was no fluke either, the Wanderers outplaying their illustrious opponents in a stirring 2-2 draw at Burnden, then eclipsing them at Anfield, where goals from John McGinlay and Andy Walker produced an emphatic 2-0 victory. Then Wolves were beaten at Molineux before Rioch's men fell to Derby County at the Baseball Ground, a rather anti-climactic end to a storming run.

The stars were McGinlay and Walker, along with winger David Lee, but the rest of the squad deserve mention: 'keeper Keith Branagan, defenders Phil Brown, David Burke, Mark Seagraves, Mark Winstanley and Alan Stubbs, midfielders Tony Kelly, Jason McAteer and Julian Darby, forwards Mark Patterson and Scott Green - they all played significant parts.

Proudly ensconced back in the First Division - albeit only the modern version, the equivalent of the former second flight - the Trotters had realistic hopes of going one better in 1993/94 and

taking their longed-for place among the Premier Division elite. But despite playing some of the brightest, neatest football to be seen anywhere in the land, their League campaign never took off. The side rarely

nudged above the table's midway point, and most of late spring was spent entrenched in the bottom half.

However, although this failure to live up to their undoubted potential in the bread-and-butter competiton was acutely

TONY PHILLISKIRK
1989/90 - 1992/93

Tony Philliskirk played what was probably the best football of his career in a three-season stint as a Trotter. Signed from Preston North End for £50,000 in June 1989, the lanky Wearsider was paired with fellow striker David Reeves, another newcomer, and immediately struck up a profitable understanding. That first term in harness, during which the Wanderers narrowly missed out on promotion from the Third Division, the pair netted 34 times, with Tony contributing 23 (including five penalties). The chemistry seemed right: the rather slow-moving but aerially effective Philliskirk, who was capable of surprising delicacy with his left foot, being complemented by the industrious Reeves, who would never be so prolific but did much of the spadework for his partner. In terms both of goals and League position, the 1990/91 campaign was almost a carbon copy of the previous one, but there was a sense that, though the duo had done reasonably well, they were not *quite* good enough. Accordingly, when there was a marked decline in 1991/92 despite the arrival of Scottish marksman Andy Walker, the crowd was on the back of Tony, who was not an obvious workhorse. It seemed a change of clubs was the likely outcome and that feeling heightened when Phil Neal, who had brought the best out of the former England schoolboy international, left the club in the spring. Sure enough, that October Tony joined Peterborough United in an £85,000 deal. He could look back on a creditable Burnden Park tenure in which he had been leading scorer in two full seasons out of three. He returned to the north-west in 1994, where he helped Burnley to promotion from division two.

disappointing, there was mammoth consolation to be found in the most exhilarating FA Cup run since the Lofthouse heyday.

It all began unpromisingly enough in a romantic but distinctly uncomfortable confrontation with Northern Premier League Gretna. The plucky Black-and-Whites had been drawn at home, but opted to switch the game from their 3,000-capacity Raydale Park, preferring the guarantee of more

lucrative gate returns at Burnden. But having made that concession, they made no more and, in front of nearly 6,500 fans, came agonisingly close to carrying the day. Twice Gretna led and they were only 11 minutes away from what would have been the greatest achievement in their history, only for two late close-range efforts from Owen Coyle to see the favourites to safety.

Bolton's first equaliser had come from the penalty spot, courtesy of John McGinlay.

The second round threw up another potentially awkward task at Third Division Lincoln, where once more the Wanderers were made to battle mightily before going through. This time they started well enough, with Alan Thompson firing them ahead with a 20-yarder after 23 minutes, but

nine minutes later the Red Imps were on level terms. Thereafter Bolton buzzed impressively, but it was not until the 69th minute that they broke through again, Phil Brown doing the damage with a spectacular, dipping long-range half-volley. Coyle's goal 120 seconds after the restart quashed any further resistance and the Trotters had secured their place alongside the

MARK PATTERSON 1990/91 -

Mark Patterson is a ferret of a footballer. He slaves selflessly on the left flank of midfield, chasing, harrying and tackling for the common good, winning the ball and using it sensibly. He chips in with the occasional priceless goal, too, such as the FA Cup third-round equaliser at home to Everton in January 1994, when he pounced on a loose ball to secure a replay. During that marvellous Cup campaign, Mark was very much the unsung hero of the Wanderers midfield as plaudits rained on Messrs McAteer, Kelly and Lee. But if he tends to be ignored by the media, his manager has no doubts about his immense value to the team; Bruce Rioch made him vice-captain to Phil Brown, safe in the knowledge that the level-headed Lancastrian would never let anyone down. Sadly, Bolton's progress towards Wembley was halted when a wayward Patterson back-pass let in Oldham's Darren Beckford to score the only goal of the quarter-final, but no one held it against a man who had striven so ceaselessly to get the Trotters so far. Mark arrived at Burnden in January 1990, a £65,000 acquisition from Bury, having already contributed solid spells to Blackburn Rovers and Preston North End. Soon he was showing the skill to go past opponents, but a lack of outright pace underlined the fact that an unquenchable work rate was the premier Patterson asset. His was a stalwart presence as Bolton were promoted from the new Second Division in 1992/93, then he went on to hold his own in the First. Mark remains an excellent clubman, ever-ready to help the youngsters, and seems a natural candidate to become a coach in the (still distant) future.

big boys in the third-round draw.

   Now the drama began with a vengeance. The little wooden ball bearing Bolton's number came out of the bag followed immediately by that of Everton, setting up a Lancashire derby which evoked memories of the conquest of Liverpool a year earlier. What would have been a sumptuous prospect under any circumstances was given added spice because it

was to be Mike Walker's first match in charge of Everton, and when Paul Rideout put the Blues ahead a minute before the interval, the new manager's first half-time pep talk was given the ideal boost. But two minutes into the second period Mark Patterson equalised with a low shot after Paul Holmes had turned the ball against his own crossbar and, thereafter, Rioch's

Stoke C.	02.85	20	0	0
Tranmere Rov.	10.85	12	0	0
Manchester C.	03.86	6	0	0
Blackpool	08.86	110	0	0
Stockport Co.	06.89	21	0	0
Hartlepool U.	03.90	11	0	0
West Bromwich A. (N/C)	08.90			
Carlisle U.	11.90	24	0	0
Chester C.	07.91	9	0	0
Preston N.E. (N/C)	11.92	1	0	0

SIMM, John
Ashton0in0Makerfield, 24 November, 1929

Bolton W.	10.47	1	0	0
Bury	05.51	47	0	8
Bradford C.	03.55	95	0	22

SLEIGHT, Geoffrey
Royston, 20 June, 1943

Bolton W.	08.61	2	0	0

SMITH, Alexander
Lancaster, 29 October, 1938

Accrington St.	08.61			
Bolton W.	03.62	19	0	0
Halifax T.	01.68	341	0	0
Preston N. E.	05.76	8	0	0

SMITH, Brian
Bolton, 12 September, 1955

Bolton W.	09.73	43	6	3
Bradford C.	10.77	8	0	0
Blackpool	08.79	18	1	1
Bournemouth	12.80	40	0	2
Bury	03.82	6	0	0

SMITH, Stephen
Huddersfield, 28 April, 1946

Huddersfield T.	10.63	330	12	30
Bolton W.	12.74	3	0	0
Halifax T.	08.77	78	3	4

SNOOKES, Eric
Birmingham, 6 March, 1955

Preston N. E.	03.73	20	0	0
Crewe Alex.	07.74	33	1	0
Southport	07.75	106	4	2
Rochdale	07.78	183	0	1
Bolton W.	07.83	6	0	0

SPOONER, Nicholas Michael
Manchester, 5 June, 1971

Bolton W.	07.89	21	1	2

STANLEY, Graham
Sheffield, 27 January, 1938

Bolton W.	10.55	141	0	3
Tranmere Rov.	07.65	0	1	1

STEVENS, Dennis
Dudley, 30 November, 1933

Bolton W.	12.50	273	0	90
Everton	03.62	120	0	20
Oldham Ath.	12.65	33	0	0
Tranmere Rov.	03.67	28	3	3

STEVENS, Ian David
Malta, 21 October, 1966

men poured forward in search of a richly deserved winner.

It was not to come but, bearing in mind the circumstances of the Liverpool knockout in 1992/93 - a home draw followed by victory away - the Burnden Park faithful were not disheartened. However, even the most buoyant of the Bolton contingent who had travelled hopefully down the East Lancs road must have been despairing after 46 minutes of the Goodison Park replay: Everton were two Stuart Barlow goals to the good and evidently in the mood to consolidate.

But hope was rekindled when the irrepressible McGinlay converted a right-wing cross from Lee on 52 minutes and then, just seven minutes from time, up popped Merseysider Alan Stubbs to capitalise on confusion between Neville Southall and Gary Ablett to tap in from ten yards. As the tie moved into extra time, the force was with the visitors, and after 100 minutes Coyle latched on to a pass from McAteer, cut inside and curled in a splendid winner.

Thus, for the second successive season, Bolton were hailed as giant-killers. It was the sort of result that would be the highlight of most seasons for most clubs, but Bruce Rioch and his attractive team were not satisfied. They had measured themselves once more against their supposed betters and had not been found wanting. Now they were eager for more scalps, a

feeling reflected all over the town as spirits were lifted by the unique excitement and glamour that a Cup run engenders.

Rioch himself positively revelled in the situation, attracting favourable national attention, not only for the flowing football of his side and their success, but also for the refreshingly matter-of-fact manner in which he handled the glare of

---

ALAN STUBBS 1990/91 -

Anyone looking for weaknesses in Alan Stubbs' game during the early months of 1994 was liable to get eye-strain - and all to no avail. Of course, at 22, the Liverpool-born central defender still had a deal to learn, yet the feeling inside football was that it was only a matter of time before he reached the very top. A boyhood Everton fan who graduated through Bolton's youth ranks, Alan presented one major initial problem to manager Phil Neal - where to play him. At the back he was very much in the immaculate mould of Alan Hansen, comfortable and cultured on the ball, a constructive passer, good in the air and crisp in the tackle; meanwhile, in midfield, his vision, stamina and powerful shot could prove invaluable. In the end he plumped for the rearguard role in which he tasted senior action for the first time in August 1990, and by the following spring he was a regular. Alan made rapid strides over the next two seasons, his only perceptible weakness being a certain casualness on the ball, which resulted occasionally in losing possession with disastrous results. But he worked hard to eradicate that flaw and, with his burgeoning natural ability underpinned by an even temperament, it was inevitable that he would become one of the most sought-after young defenders in the land. That duly happened during Bolton's high-profile FA Cup run in 1993/94, after which he was called into the full England squad and awarded a 'B' cap. Terry Venables, with wise understatement, said: 'It's early days for Alan, but he looks a fair player.' Liverpool were rumoured to have had a £2 million-plus bid turned down in early summer, while for his part, Alan appeared happy to remain at Burnden and strive to realise his Premiership ambitions with Bolton. What a wonderful thought!

Preston N. E.	11.84	9	2	2
Stockport Co. (N/C)	10.86	1	1	0
Bolton W.	03.87	26	21	7
Bury	07.91	100	10	38

STORER, Stuart John
Rugby, 16 January, 1967

Mansfield T. (YT)	08.83	0	1	0
Birmingham C.	01.85	5	3	0
Everton	03.87			
Wigan Ath.	07.87	9	3	0
Bolton W.	12.87	95	28	12
Exeter C.	03.93	54	0	6

STUBBS, Alan
Liverpool, 6 October, 1971

Bolton W.	07.90	120	18	4

SUTTON, David William
Tarleton (Lancs), 21 January, 1957

Plymouth Arg.	07.74	60	1	0
Reading	11.77	9	0	0
Huddersfield T.	03.78	242	0	11
Bolton W.	06.85	98	0	4
Rochdale	08.88	28	0	2

TAYLOR, Gordon
Ashton-u-Lyne, 28 December, 1944

Bolton W.	01.62	253	5	41
Birmingham C.	12.70	156	10	9
Blackburn Rov.	03.76	62	2	3
Bury	06.78	58	2	2

TAYLOR, Steven Jeffrey
Royton, 18 October, 1955

Bolton W.	10.73	34	6	16
Port Vale	10.75	4	0	2
Oldham Ath.	10.77	45	2	25
Luton T.	01.79	15	5	1
Mansfield T.	07.79	30	7	7
Burnley	07.80	80	6	37
Wigan Ath.	08.83	29	1	7
Stockport Co.	03.84	26	0	8
Rochdale	11.84	84	0	42
Preston N.E.	10.86	5	0	2
Burnley	08.87	38	7	6
Rochdale	03.89	16	1	4

THOMAS, John William
Wednesbury, 5 August, 1958

Everton	08.77			
Tranmere Rov.	03.79	10	1	2
Halifax T.	10.79	5	0	0
Bolton W.	06.80	18	4	6
Chester C.	08.82	44	0	20
Lincoln C.	08.83	56	11	18
Preston N.E.	06.85	69	9	38
Bolton W.	07.87	71	2	31
West Bromwich A.	07.89	8	10	1
Preston N.E.	02.90	24	3	6
Hartlepool U.	03.92	5	2	1
Halifax T.	07.92	10	2	0

THOMPSON, Alan
Newcastle, 22 December 1973

Newcastle U.	03.91	13	3	0
Bolton W.	08.93	19	8	6

publicity. As a former Scotland captain who had played for several top clubs, there wasn't much he hadn't seen but when he was made Bolton boss after resigning from Millwall in May 1992, not everyone who followed the Trotters was enamoured at the prospect. Some were not endeared by his reputation for ruthlessness as a player (although his skill was undeniable) and maybe they were intimidated by a military bearing, the product of an English Army upbringing. But they need not have worried: certainly he underlined the need for hard work, but he emphasised the skill factor, too, as well as fostering an admirably positive and caring attitude from *everyone* at the club. This was illustrated vividly when, as the fans queued in the cold to buy tickets for the fourth-round encounter with Arsenal at Burnden, he sent some of his players out to serve them with tea. It was a gesture as warming to the heart as to the body, and one which could hardly have

been better judged.

The Gunners, of course, represented as stiff a test as it was possible to face in knockout competition. They were holders of both major domestic cups and had not lost in the FA Cup

since January 1992. Bolton, however, were uncowed and tore into their illustrious opponents, twice going close before McGinlay set up young McAteer to slip the ball coolly under the body of David

Seaman after 31 minutes. Dame Fortune appeared to have forsaken the Wanderers' cause as Ian Wright equalised following a lucky rebound on 51 minutes, and a quarter of an hour later Tony Adams stole in to put the North Londoners in front against the run of play with a glancing header. But Bolton kept their heads, continued to play constructively and got their just deserts when Coyle netted emphatically with only four minutes remaining.

Suddenly Burnden was awash with euphoria but the task that lay ahead, a visit to Highbury, was formidable indeed. Now the smart money had to be on Arsenal but, yet again, the underdogs were not to be denied. Bolton's coach was delayed by heavy traffic on the way to the ground, and 20 minutes into the action, George Graham's team might have been wishing their sparky opponents had been held up indefinitely. By then Kevin Campbell had

missed a fine chance to put the home side in front, but the Trotters were settling ominously into their customary perky rhythm. Suddenly David Lee erupted with a thunderous 25-yarder which Seaman only just managed to push away for a corner. Patterson took the kick, there followed a bout of head-tennis which culminated in Brown finding the unmarked McGinlay who nodded in from close range.

Sixteen minutes later Alan Smith relieved the

TONY KELLY 1991/92 - 19994/95

One day, Tony Kelly might look back over his career, heave a huge sigh and say 'If only . . .' The rotund, much-travelled midfielder is slow, but blessed with such a sublime touch on the ball and such breathtaking vision that by now, at the age of 30, he should be a household name. His passes - whether stiletto-like through-balls or raking crossfield deliveries that instantly switch the angle of play - can open the most clam-like of defences, and he is a wickedly cunning striker of a dead ball. Scouser Tony is as hard as nails, too, unyielding in the most fearsome of challenges, intimidated by no one. And yet, after starting his playing days as an Anfield apprentice, he has served a succession of clubs in the lower divisions, each time giving a tantalising glimpse of his gifts and then moving on. The problem has been that Tony has not always applied himself rigidly enough to meet managers' exacting standards; his lack of pace has been accentuated by a natural tendency to put on weight; and there has been a certain rebellious streak in his make-up which, at times, has not served him well. He arrived at Burnden Park from Shrewsbury Town in August 1991 and soon it became evident that, when he was on song, Tony gave the team a different dimension. He reached a creative peak during the FA Cup run of 1993/94 when, clearly, he was fired up by the challenge of testing his talent against Premiership opposition. Combining sweetly in central midfield with the hard-running Jason McAteer, he made inspirational contributions against both Everton and Arsenal, but then, when Bolton were eliminated, he lost form and was dropped.The following autumn he joined Port Vale on a free transfer, and it seemed that time was running out if Tony was to realise anything like his full potential.

mounting pressure on Arsenal by grabbing an equaliser and the feeling that the Gunners would, after all, grind out a victory began to grow. But Bolton remained true to their pedigree once more, playing the better football throughout an entertaining second half and on into extra time. Then, finally, it was all right on the night. After 100 minutes, a woeful pass by Nigel Winterburn let in Coyle, Seaman deflected his shot against an upright only for McAteer to turn the loose ball into the net. Then an error by Arsenal's other England full-back, Lee Dixon, let in substitute Andy Walker to make the game safe with a deliciously cool cross-shot five minutes from the end.

That week Charlton Athletic had unseated Championship challengers Blackburn Rovers from the Cup, Luton Town had dumped Kevin Keegan's on-form Newcastle and Oxford United had knocked out mighty Leeds. Truly the First Division legions were rampant and the belief

took root - and nowhere more than at Burnden Park - that this could be the year for one of the less fashionable clubs to lift the famous old trophy.

Accordingly, Ron Atkinson's Aston Villa

did not relish their fifth-round assignation at Bolton - with good reason, as it turned out! In the first half of an exciting Sunday afternoon encounter, defences remained surpreme, Bolton going

110

closest to breaking the deadlock when full-back Jimmy Phillips rattled the Midlanders' bar on 36 minutes. After the break it was Villa who threatened, but two good chances went begging; then back came Bolton

and Tony Kelly almost beat 'keeper Mark Bosnich with a curling free-kick. As time ticked away, yet another replay seemed likely but just eight minutes from the final whistle, the most accomplished man afield

---

DAVID LEE 1992/93 -

On his day, David Lee is a match-winning winger extraordinaire, an entertainer who lifts a crowd every time he receives the ball. He can dash through a defence leaving a trail of standed defenders in his wake, or drop a perfect centre on to the head of John McGinlay from 40 yards, or threaten any 'keeper with his ferocious power of shot. That's when the Muse is with him. When it's not, like so many gifted wingers, he can be the most frustrating player imaginable, utterly anonymous, little more than a liability. David began his career at Bury, thrilling the Gigg Lane regulars for four seasons and attracting the attention of Manchester United and Bolton, among others. Phil Neal tried to take him to Burnden but a deal never happened and he moved to Southampton instead. David never settled on the south coast, where he was frequently confined to the substitutes' bench and in November 1992, only 15 months after checking in at The Dell, he joined the Trotters on loan. He impressed immediately and soon Bruce Rioch parted with £300,000 to make the signing permanent. For the rest of the season, David continued to do well, often linking effectively with Andy Walker. He starred in the 2-0 FA Cup knockout of Liverpool at Anfield, creating the first goal for McGinlay with an exquisite cross, and expectations rose sky-high. And, to be fair, he continued to produce splendid displays into 1993/94, glittering in the FA Cup replay against Arsenal at Highbury, for example. But then his confidence, and his consistency, slipped to such an extent that, towards the end of term, he was dropped. Clearly, season 1994/95 would be crucial; getting the best out of David Lee on a regular basis was one of the most important challenges facing Bruce Rioch.

THOMPSON, Christopher David
Walsall, 24 January, 1960

Bolton W.	07.77	66	7	18
Lincoln C.	03.83	5	1	0
Blackburn Rov.	08.83	81	4	24
Wigan Ath.	07.86	67	7	12
Blackpool	07.88	27	12	8
Cardiff C.	03.90	1	1	0
Walsall (N/C)	02.91	3	0	0

THOMPSON, Peter
Carlisle, 27 November, 1942

Preston N.E.	11.59	121	0	20
Liverpool		318	4	41
Bolton W.	11.73	111	6	2

THOMPSON, Stephen James
Oldham, 2 November, 1964

Bolton W.	11.82	329	6	49
Luton T.	09.91	5	0	0
Leicester C.	10.91	105	3	18

THRELFALL, John
Little Lever, 22 March, 1935(FB)

Bolton W.	12.54	47	0	1
Bury	11.62	37	0	1

THRELFALL, J. Richard
Ashton, 5 March, 1916

Bolton W.	07.45	3	0	0
Halifax T.	10.47	30	0	0

TRAIN, Raymond
Nuneaton, 10 February, 1951

Walsall	11.68	67	6	11
Carlisle U.	12.71	154	1	8
Sunderland	03.76	31	1	1
Bolton W.	03.77	49	2	0
Watford	11.78	91	1	3
Oxford U.	03.82	49	1	0
Bournemouth	11.83	7	0	0
Northampton T.	03.84	46	0	1
Tranmere Rov.	08.85	36	0	0
Walsall	08.86	16	0	0

VALENTINE, Peter
Huddersfield, 16 April, 1963

Huddersfield T.	04.81	19	0	1
Bolton W.	07.83	66	2	1
Bury	07.85	314	5	16
Carlisle U.	08.93	18	2	2

WALDRON, Alan
Royton, 6 September, 1951

Bolton W.	09.69	127	14	6
Blackpool	12.77	22	1	1
Bury	06.79	34	0	0
York C.	09.81	3	0	1

WALKER, Andrew F.
Glasgow, 6 April, 1965

Newcastle U. (L)	09.91	2	0	0
Bolton W.	01.92	61	6	44

WALKER, Roger A.
Bolton, 15 November, 1966

Bolton W.	07.85	7	5	1

on the day, Trotters central defender Alan Stubbs, strode forward to take a decisive role. Brushing aside team-mate Kelly - after all, he'd had his chance! - Stubbs struck a low 20-yard free-kick past Bosnich for the only goal of the game. Thus Bolton had preserved a record, dating back 20 years and 18 games, of not losing on a Sunday,

Jason McAteer (left) celebrates Bolton's 1994 FA Cup victory at Highbury with John McGinlay (centre) and Andy Walker.

JOHN McGINLAY 1992/93 -

Spirited Highlander John McGinlay is a late developer who, at the age of 30, achieved a truly superb standard of all-round centre-forward play for Bolton in 1993/94. Despite the date on his birth certificate, he was coveted by many of the most eminent clubs in the land, and his progress was recognised by a belated call-up for Scotland. John has all the attributes demanded of a traditional leader of the line. His control enables him to lay the ball off neatly while he is strong enough to retain possession in the face of heavy challenges, but it is his ability to find the net that most delights the fans. Excellent in the air, and blessed with a powerful and accurate shot, he carries constant menace and his 33 goals in all competitions during his *annus mirabilis* equalled the club record held jointly by Nat Lofthouse and Andy Walker. In addition, he exudes an indomitable fervour reminiscent of his countryman Andy Gray's, which frequently lifts the men around him to new heights. In his young days at Elgin City and Yeovil Town, John was too immature to make the most of his talent. He went on to score prolifically enough for his first two League employers, Shrewsbury and Bury, without attracting a top club. There followed a stint at Millwall, where he was managed by Bruce Rioch, who understood his full potential and was happy to pay £125,000 to make him a Trotter in September 1992. John responded with some memorable displays that term, notably in the glorious FA Cup victory at Anfield, where he nodded a princely goal from David Lee's cross. Even better followed, and who is to say the very best of John McGinlay is not still to come?

ANDY WALKER 1991/92 - 1993/94

When Andy Walker is fully fit and on song, it's difficult to think of a more lethal finisher in British football. If the ball reaches the slim Glaswegian in the penalty box, then no defence is safe. His first touch is deadly - he can turn an opponent with a single deft movement - but it is Andy's final touch that carries most menace. He is an opportunist, a 'sniffer', who can dispatch chances with clinical aplomb. True, he is not powerful in the air, preferring to feed off titbits from the likes of John McGinlay, but such is the Walker efficiency on the deck that there were few complaints following his arrival at Burnden in January 1992. That, in itself, was unexpected, Phil Neal taking him on loan after he had failed to fit in with the plans of new Celtic boss Liam Brady, and a loan stint at Newcastle had come to nothing. Andy said 'hello' by rising from the bench at Exeter to score within two minutes of taking the pitch. Thereafter, the Scottish international - who won his sole cap in 1988 - could do no wrong. During the remainder of that season he notched 15 goals from 24 outings, then established himself as Burnden's latest folk hero in 1992/93, netting 33 times in senior competition to equal the club record for one term held by Nat Lofthouse. But then, just as the former 'Bhoy' was being scrutinised by his national boss, Andy Roxburgh, he was cut off in full flow, damaging his cruciate ligament against Swansea in mid-April. Thus Andy missed out on the promotion party and was sidelined until the New Year. However, he regained fitness and signalled his return with a coolly taken goal to kill off Arsenal at Highbury and hopes were high that he would be back to his best in 1994/95. But, sadly, Andy rejoined Celtic for a barely adequate, tribunal-set £550,000 fee in the summer. Some said he was too relaxed, others that he was too fiery, but that was all part of the irresistible Walker cocktail.

113

but more importantly, they were in the quarter-finals of the FA Cup. Now the football world at large began to acknowledge that, yes, there might be some measure of reality in the half-whispered hopes that this might indeed be Bolton Wanderers' year to shine. Most of the big clubs were out of contention and the dream took shape: a sunny day in May, the Trotters against, say, Manchester United at Wembley. That had the perfect ring and, after all, it had happened before.

However, come sixth-round day and, somehow, there was a whiff of doom in the air. It was dreary and drizzly; the Burnden Park pitch was sandy, muddy, messy, not the ideal surface for good football; and the opponents, Premier League strugglers Oldham Athletic, hardly exuded glamour. Bolton found themselves in the unaccustomed position of favourites in the judgement of many pundits and, to be fair, their display justified such confidence. They looked the likeliest to

score throughout the game and if Mark Seagraves' early drive against the bar had been a few inches lower, or if the referee had awarded a penalty when Coyle was checked by Richard Jobson, then the

outcome might have been so different. But such is football and, while it was Oldham who looked like lower division scrappers as they hustled ceaselessly to negate the midfield creativity of Kelly and

114

McAteer, Joe Royle's team showed remarkable resilience. As the afternoon wore on, it seemed increasingly likely that one mistake would settle the outcome, and so it proved. It fell to poor Mark Patterson to drop the clanger, misjudging a back-pass seven minutes from time which freed Darren Beckford to slot home the only goal, just about the only thing he had done right all afternoon.

JASON McATEER 1992/93 -

Making extravagant claims about young players can be unfair and counter-productive, but after watching Jason McAteer for a season and a half, most Bolton fans were finding it difficult not to wax lyrical. Their enthusiasm was understandable. The personable Merseysider was shaping up as the complete modern midfielder, ferrying constantly back and forth between penalty areas, tackling crisply, passing accurately and running, running, running. Jason, the nephew of former British and Empire middleweight boxing champion Pat McAteer, was signed from the HFS Loans Premier League club Marine for £500 plus the promise of a friendly match. That followed a trial in which he had been anonymous in the first half but electric in the second, playing on the right wing and showing the skill and control to nip past defenders. Jason's senior debut came as a substitute at home to Burnley in November 1992, and not long afterwards he was ensconced as a regular. National acclaim built up during the FA Cup run of 1993/94, especially after his two performances against Arsenal, each of which were embellished with a goal. Because he is so mobile, Jason is almost impossible to shackle, as specialist man-marker Martin Keown discovered at Highbury, where the 22-year-old led him a merry dance. In March, the ever-improving McAteer made another giant step towards stardom when Jack Charlton picked him for the Republic of Ireland, and he went on to impress in the World Cup Finals. Inevitably, Jason's name was linked with a succession of Premiership clubs, but at the time of writing there was hope that his awesome potential might be allowed to continue its development at Burnden Park, at least for the immediate future.

WALSH, Michael Thomas
Manchester, 20 June, 1956

Bolton W.	07.74	169	8	4
Everton	08.81	20	0	0
Norwich C.	10.82	5	0	0
Burnley	12.82	3	0	0
Manchester C.	10.83	3	1	0
Blackpool	02.84	146	7	5
Bury	07.89			

WALTON, Mark Andrew
Merthyr Tydfil, 1 June, 1969

Luton T.	02.87			
Colchester U.	11.87	40	0	0
Norwich C.	08.89	22	0	0
Wrexham	08.93	6	0	0
Bolton W.	03.94	3	0	0

WEBSTER, Harold
Sheffield, 22 August, 1930

Bolton W.	10.48	98	0	38
Chester C.	06.58	34	0	11

WESTWOOD, Raymond William
Brierley Hill, 14 April, 1912   Died 1982

Bolton W.	03.30	301	0	127
Chester C.	12.47	39	0	13

WHARTON, Terence John
Bolton, 1 July, 1942

Wolverhampton W.	10.59	223	1	69
Bolton W.	11.67	101	1	28
Crystal Palace	01.71	19	1	1
Walsall	11.73	1	0	0

WHATMORE, Neil
Ellesmere Port, 17 May, 1955

Bolton W.	05.73	262	15	102
Birmingham C.	08.81	24	2	6
Bolton W.	12.82	10	0	3
Oxford U.	02.83	33	3	15
Bolton W.	03.84	7	0	2
Burnley	08.84	8	0	1
Mansfield T.	11.84	71	1	20
Bolton W.	08.87			
Mansfield T. (N/C)	11.87	0	4	0

WHEELER, John Edward
Liverpool, 26 July, 1928

Tranmere Rov.	04.46	101	0	9
Bolton W.	02.51	189	0	18
Liverpool	09.56	164	0	21

WHITTAKER, Stuart
Liverpool, 2 January, 1975

Bolton W.	05.93	2	0	0

WHITWORTH, Stephen
Coalville, 20 March, 1952

Leicester C.	11.69	352	1	0
Sunderland	03.79	83	0	0
Bolton W.	10.81	67	0	0
Mansfield T.	08.83	80	0	2

WILKINSON, Roy Joseph
Hiendley Green, 17 September, 1941

Bolton W.	02.60	3	0	0

This was bitter gruel for the Wanderers to stomach but Rioch managed a philosophical reaction: 'We're disappointed but the players have earned a tremendous amount of appreciation and respect through their efforts. Unfortunately, we have dropped a lot of League points since the Cup run got going.' In fact, with nine out of the remaining 13 League games at home, Bolton still held out some hope of reaching the promotion play-offs, but it was not to be. A final position in lower mid-table was not much to show for such an enterprising season, but there were distinct pluses. The high profile of the club had helped secure first full international caps for 30-year-old John McGinlay, who scored on his debut for Scotland, and for Jason McAteer and Owen Coyle, who both made appearances for the Republic of Ireland. In addition Alan Stubbs, along with McAteer the subject of much transfer speculation, was called by Terry Venables into the England squad and he looks a player with a illustrious future.

Rioch himself was linked with Premiership employers, but by the summer of 1994 it was a rare Trotters fan who was not hoping against hope that Bruce would remain. The club appeared to be on the rise, and plans for a move to a new custom-built stadium two miles west of town had been mooted. Remarkably, sentimentalists who regretted any break with the Wanderers' Burnden heritage appeared outnumbered by pragmatists who saw

OWEN COYLE 1993/94 -

Owen Coyle is a slim dart of a striker whose stiletto thrusts were a highlight of Bolton's exhilarating 1994 FA Cup run. Two second-half strikes to spare the Wanderers' blushes against little Gretna, a goal at Lincoln, the winner in the replay at Everton and a late equaliser at home to Arsenal - they added up to a momentous contribution to one of the most exciting sequences in the club's modern history. Yet it has not been all sweetness and light for Owen following his £250,000 move from Airdrieonians in the summer of 1993. At first he seemed ill at ease in English football and, before long, he found the crowd on his back. However, his transformation of the Gretna game won them over and soon they were chanting for him whenever he was not in the team. As he grew in confidence, Owen revealed an enviable range of abilities. He showed speed, good control and accuracy of shot under pressure, but most gratifying of all was his knack of turning past defenders when space was tight. Sometimes, it must be admitted, he tended to take one turn too many and run into unnecessary trouble, and that is an aspect of his play on which Messrs Rioch and Todd can be expected to work. Such was Owen's progress during his first campaign as a Trotter that he won full international recognition with the Republic of Ireland and narrowly missed a trip to the United States for the World Cup. Of course, with several accomplished marksmen pushing for a place alongside John McGinlay, there is always going to be hot competition for a front role at Bolton and towards the end of 1993/94 Owen found himself out of the side. A spirited reaction was expected in 1994/95.

new headquarters as the ideal foundation for a fresh start. With such an attitude holding sway, and with so much of the hard work towards building a successful team apparently completed, there seemed to be ample inducement for Bruce Rioch to stay and finish the job he had started so promisingly.

WILLIAMS, Gareth Cyril
Hendon, 30 October, 1941

Cardiff C.	04.59	161	0	14
Bolton W.	10.67	108	1	11
Bury	10.71	39	3	4

WILSON, Philip
Hemsworth, 16 October, 1960

Bolton W.	10.78	35	4	4
Huddersfield T.	08.81	229	4	16
York C.	08.87	38	8	2
Scarborough (N/C)	12.89	39	4	1

WINSTANLEY, Mark Andrew
St Helens, 22 January, 1968

Bolton W.	07.86	215	5	3

WINTER, Daniel Thomas
Tonypandy, 14 June, 1918

Bolton W.	06.35	34	0	0
Chelsea	12.45	131	0	0

WOODWARD, Thomas
Westhoughton, 8 December, 1917

Bolton W.	01.35	152	0	18
Middlesbrough	10.49	19	0	6

WORTHINGTON, Frank Stewart
Halifax, 23 November, 1948

Huddersfield T.	11.66	166	5	41
Leicester C.	08.72	209	1	72
Bolton W.	09.77	81	3	35
Birmingham C.	11.79	71	4	29
Leeds U.	03.82	32	0	14
Sunderland	12.82	18	1	2
Southampton	06.83	34	0	4
Brighton & H.A.	05.84	27	4	7
Tranmere Rov.	06.85	51	8	21
Preston N.E.	02.87	10	13	3
Stockport Co.	11.87	18	1	6

WRIGGLESWORTH, William
South Elmsall, 12 November, 1912

Chesterfield	05.32	34	0	6
Wolverhampton W.	12.34	50	0	21
Manchester U.	02.37	27	0	7
Bolton W.	01.47	13	0	1
Southampton	10.47	12	0	4
Reading	06.48	5	0	0

WRIGHT, Charles George
Glasgow, 11 December, 1938

Workington	06.58	123	0	0
Grimsby T.	02.63	129	0	0
Charlton Ath.	03.66	195	0	0
Bolton W.	06.71	88	0	0

WRIGHT, Ralph Lawrence
Newcastle, 3 August, 1947

Norwich C.	07.68			
Bradford P.A.	10.69	13	1	1
Hartlepool U.	06.70	24	1	3
Stockport Co.	07.71	19	2	0
Bolton W.	02.72	25	7	5
Southport	12.72	40	3	5

BOLTON WANDERERS SEASON BY SEASON

1945/6   3rd in Wartime League (North), FA Cup semi-final
1946/7   18th in Div 1, FA Cup 4th rd
1947/8   17th in Div 1, FA Cup 3rd rd
1948/9   14th in Div 1, FA Cup 3rd rd
1949/50 16th in Div 1, FA Cup 4th rd
1950/1   8th in Div 1, FA Cup 4th rd
1951/2   5th in Div 1, FA Cup 3rd rd
1952/3   14th in Div 1, FA Cup finalists
1953/4   5th in Div 1, FA Cup quarter- final
1954/5   18th in Div 1, FA Cup 4th rd
1955/6   8th in Div 1, FA Cup 4th rd
1956/7   9th in Div 1, FA Cup 3rd rd
1957/8   15th in Div 1, FA Cup winners
1958/9   4th in Div 1, FA Cup quarter-final
1959/60 6th in Div 1, FA Cup 4th rd
1960/1   18th in Div 1, FA Cup 4th rd, League Cup 4th rd
1961/2   11th in Div 1, FA Cup 3rd rd, League Cup 1st rd
1962/3   18th in Div 1, FA Cup 3rd rd, League Cup 2nd rd
1963/4   21st in Div 1, FA Cup 4th rd, League Cup 3rd rd
1964/5   3rd in Div 2, FA Cup 5th rd, League Cup 2nd rd
1965/6   9th in Div 2, FA Cup 4th rd, League Cup 3rd rd
1966/7   9th in Div 2, FA Cup 4th rd, League Cup 2nd rd
1967/8   12th in Div 2, FA Cup 3rd rd, League Cup 3rd rd
1968/9   17th in Div 2, FA Cup 4th rd, League Cup 2nd rd
1969/70 16th in Div 2, FA Cup 3rd rd, League Cup 2nd rd
1970/71 22nd in Div 2, FA Cup 3rd rd, League Cup 3rd rd
1971/2   7th in Div 3, FA Cup 4th rd, League Cup 4th rd
1972/3   1st in Div 3, FA Cup 5th rd, League Cup 2nd rd

1973/4 11th in Div 2, FA Cup 4th rd, League Cup 3rd rd

1974/5 10th in Div 2, FA Cup 3rd rd, League Cup 2nd rd

1975/6 4th in Div 2, FA Cup 5th rd, League Cup 2nd rd

1976/7 4th in Div 2, FA Cup 3rd rd, League Cup semi-final

1977/8 1st in Div 2, FA Cup 5th rd, League Cup 4th rd

1978/9 17th in Div 1, FA Cup 3rd rd, League Cup 3rd rd

1979/80 22nd in Div 1, FA Cup 5th rd, League Cup 2nd rd

1980/1 18th in Div 2, FA Cup 3rd rd, League Cup 2nd rd

1981/2 19th in Div 2, FA Cup 4th rd, League Cup 1st rd

1982/3 22nd in Div 2, FA Cup 3rd rd, League Cup 2nd rd

1983/4 10th in Div 3, FA Cup 3rd rd, League Cup 1st rd

1984/5 17th in Div 3, FA Cup 1st rd, League Cup 3rd rd

1985/6 18th in Div 3, FA Cup 1st rd, League Cup 2nd rd, Freight Rover Cup finalists

1986/7 21st in Div 3 (lost in play-offs), FA Cup 3rd rd, League Cup 1st rd

1987/8 3rd in Div 4, FA Cup 3rd rd, League Cup 1st rd

1988/9 10th in Div 3, FA Cup 2nd rd, League Cup 1st rd, Sherpa Van Trophy winners

1989/90 6th in Div 3 (lost in play-offs), FA Cup 1st rd, League Cup 3rd rd

1990/1 4th in Div 3 (lost in play-offs), FA Cup 4th rd, League Cup 2nd rd

1991/2 13th in Div 3, FA Cup 5th rd, League Cup 2nd rd

1992/3 2nd in New Div 2, FA Cup 5th rd, League Cup 2nd rd

1993/4 14th in New Div 1, FA Cup quarter-final, League Cup 2nd rd

BOLTON MANAGERS

Walter Rowley Aug 44 - Oct 50
Bill Ridding Oct 50 - Feb 51 (caretaker), Feb 51 - Aug 68
Nat Lofthouse Aug 68 - Dec 68 (caretaker), Dec 68 - Nov 70
Jimmy McIlroy Nov 70 (for 18 days)
Nat Lofthouse Nov 70 - Jan 71
Jimmy Meadows Jan - April 71
Nat Lofthouse April - May 71
Jimmy Armfield May 71 - Oct 74
Ian Greaves Oct 74 - Jan 80
Stan Anderson Feb 80 - May 81
George Mulhall June 81 - June 82
John McGovern June 82 - Jan 85
Charlie Wright Feb - Dec 85
Nat Lofthouse Dec 85 (caretaker)
Phil Neal Dec 85 - May 92
Bruce Rioch May 92 -